North Carolina Haunts

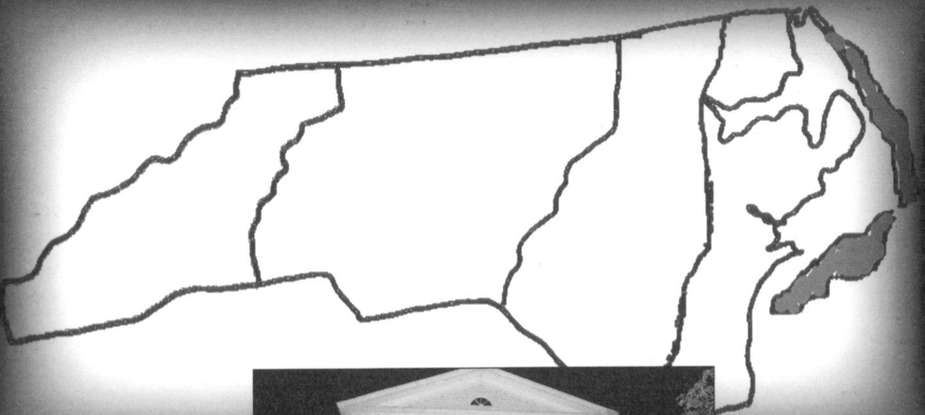

Kevin Ward

Schiffer Publishing Ltd

4880 Lower Valley Road, Atglen, Pennsylvania 19310

Dedication

To my beloved mother Mary Russell Ward

When sick she nursed me through the night
Through the darkest hours until the new dawn's light

She cheered me up when I was sad
Forgave me when I acted bad

So now because she feels my pain
She's come to help me once again…
— Gordon Finnegan (sinisterfin)

Schiffer Books are available at special discounts for bulk purchases for sales promotions or premiums. Special editions, including personalized covers, corporate imprints, and excerpts can be created in large quantities for special needs. For more information contact the publisher:

Published by Schiffer Publishing Ltd.
4880 Lower Valley Road
Atglen, PA 19310
Phone: (610) 593-1777; Fax: (610) 593-2002
E-mail: Info@schifferbooks.com

For the largest selection of fine reference books on this and related subjects,
please visit our website at: **www.schifferbooks.com**
We are always looking for people to write books on new and related subjects.
If you have an idea for a book please contact us at the above address.

This book may be purchased from the publisher.
Include $5.00 for shipping.
Please try your bookstore first.
You may write for a free catalog.

In Europe, Schiffer books are distributed by
Bushwood Books
6 Marksbury Ave.
Kew Gardens
Surrey TW9 4JF England
Phone: 44 (0) 20 8392 8585; Fax: 44 (0) 20 8392 9876
E-mail: info@bushwoodbooks.co.uk
Website: www.bushwoodbooks.co.uk

Designed by Mark David Bowyer
Type set in Burton's Nightmare 2000 / New Baskerville BT

ISBN: 978-0-7643-3790-1
Printed in the United States of America

Contents

Acknowledgments 4
Introduction 5
My Story 7

Chapter One: The Mountains 17
Samuel Reed House 17
Battery Park Hotel 20
Smith McDowell House 23
Grove Park Inn 28
Brown Mountain Lights.......................... 31
1927 Lake Lure Inn 34
Old Wilkes Jail 40

Chapter Two: The Piedmont 44
The Capitol Building 44
Mordecai House 50
Queens College 53
McAlpine Park... 56
The Cajun Queen 58
Gimghoul Castle 61
The Carolina Inn 63
Latta Plantation...................................... 65
Piney Grove Church 72
The Devil's Tramping Ground 75
Victor Small House 78

Chapter Three: The Coastal Plains 81
Stonewall Manor 81
MacHaven 90
The Prince Charles Hotel....................... 94
The Kyle House.. 98
The Bentonville Battleground.............. 100
Janet Brinkley...................................... 105

Chapter Four: Coastal Tidewater 110
The Battleship North Carolina 110
The Cotton Exchange............................ 118
Maco Lights... 125
Orton's 128
Level Five... 132
Fort Fisher... 133
Nell Cropsey House 141

Chapter Five: The Outer Banks 145
The *Carroll A. Deering*.......................145
Blackbeard 150
Cape Hatteras 156

Acknowledgments

This book would not have been possible without the help of so many terrific folks. I would like to thank those who shared their stories, like Jason Camp, Matt DaVita, and their team C.S.P.O.T (Carolina Supernatural Phenomena), which shared some of their cases from the Wilmington area with me. Additionally, I would like to thank Kimberly M. Kenyon and her team Southern Spooks, as they were also kind enough to share some of their investigations.

The staff and management of various historical sites were extremely helpful to me as well: Lisa Whitfield, the education director of the Smith-McDowell house, shared the history of the famous home and cases of the paranormal; Tiffianna Honsinger, and the entire education staff of the State Capitol building, let me use stories that they had collected through the decades; Kristin Toler, from Latta Plantation, was extremely helpful and provided countless stories from the plantation's rich history. Special thanks to the late T. E. Ricks and his meticulous collection of paranormal occurrences at Stone Wall Manor and Lauren Filliettaz for sharing Mr. Ricks's stories with me.

For the help of people like my good friend Stephen Smith and my wonderful sister Lisa Ward for editing my work. Also I would like to thank my entire family and all of my friends — they have always been very supportive of me.

I would also like to thank Dinah Roseberry and Schiffer Publishing for allowing me to write this book and giving me the opportunity to tell my mom about it...only weeks before she passed on to the next life.

Finally I would very much like to thank God who makes all things possible!

Introduction

I have been a lifelong resident of North Carolina; I have lived all across the state in my life and have enjoyed every place I called home in the Tar Heel state. I am, in the long view of time a late comer, to this proud Southern State, people have called this land home long before me, and in fact many called it home before the first Europeans landed here. It was home to native tribes like the Catawba and the Cherokee, who had much respect and love for the land that would eventually become the state I now call home.

It is not a stretch to say that North Carolina was first established with a certain bit of the mysterious to it. As any good North Carolinian worth their salt will tell you, one of the first attempts by British settlers at a permanent colony, the now very infamous Roanoke colony, disappeared in 1590, leaving behind only the word "Croatan" carved in a nearby tree. Although there are countless theories, no one has ever found the definitive answer to what happened to the nearly 149 colonists who simply vanished. Certainly this is an ominous way for the relationship between this land and European settlers to start on.

Since the disappearance of those British colonists, North Carolina has been the site of many important moments in America's history. During the later days of the Revolution in 1781, American General Nathan Greene engaged the British general Cornwallis at the battle of Guilford Courthouse in modern day Greensboro. The Tar Heel state also served as host to several battles of the American Civil War. The Battle of Bentonville and Fort Fisher, both of which came late in the War Between the States, were sites that witnessed great loss of life on both.

Those are just some of the moments that make up this great state's history. Events like the first flight of the Wright brothers in 1903 or the birth of two American Presidents (James K. Polk, Andrew Johnson) are among other things we can rightfully call our own.

Now, along with this history, comes what some would call folklore and other say is fact, ghost, spirits, poltergeist. Whatever you prefer to call them, many people throughout the state's history have reported encounters with these ethereal beings from the Mountains to the Outer Banks; they have been seen all across it.

During my life, I have lived in two houses that I am positive were haunted: one when I was a young boy in Rocky Mount, the other as a teenager in Fayetteville. Actually experiencing ghosts firsthand made me a believer at a very young age; I soon began reading everything I could about the supernatural and anything to do with paranormal investigation.

The more I read about haunted places across the world the more I really wanted to see them and hear stories about them from the people who actually experienced them. Even though I was unable to tour the globe on a ghost hunting expedition I was able to find the places in my own state that had its share of the spectral touch.

I have never had a problem declaring my belief about ghosts to anyone who cared to listen regardless of whether they agreed or thought I was completely off my rocker, so in response to this honest assertion of belief, many people would share their own encounters with me. More people then I would have ever imaged had their own amazing stories to share with me concerning phantom children, deceased family members coming back to let everyone know they were okay, or just noisy specters causing a fuss in people's homes. Some of these encounters seemed, in general, terrifying while others seemed almost good natured or even comforting, which helped show the spectrum of paranormal activity that is all around.

As I began to realize that I was not alone (and how much so) I was in experiencing the supernatural, I felt, with increasing confidence, that I could talk about it in the public venues, because more people than not seemed to be open to the possibilities.

I have never been an official paranormal investigator and, although I have dabbled in it now and then, I have no desire in asking spirits to perform for me on cue. I believe the best accounts of ghosts come from those who have been in a home for an extended time, or a place that has visitors present for large parts of the day. For the most part, I think this is because why ever these wandering spirits are still doing here on earth; they seem to only be capable of brief moments of making their presence known to the living, so effectually, the more people are around the better chance of it being noticed.

North Carolina, from the mountains to the Outer Banks, is filled with historic sites or private residences that seem to have their fair share of ghosts lingering around, for whatever reason. I was very glad to have so many people across the state share their stories with me so that I could include them in this book. I have heard so many shocking encounters with the paranormal from many places and, while these make up barely even a fraction of the haunted locations in North Carolina, they are among some of the most fascinating.

My Story

I am a firm believer in the paranormal and not because I want to be or that I have a particularly open mind — I actually have witnessed the paranormal for myself when I was a young child. It is fair to say that I was never given a chance to be skeptical about the supernatural world. After my childhood experience at my home in Rocky Mount, North Carolina, I became acutely aware and developed a lifelong interest in the supernatural.

It was the late 1980s. I lived with my parents and siblings — my two sisters Lisa and Susan and my two brothers Troy and Michael — in an older house on Sunset Avenue. We had been living in the house for two years and had found it to be a pleasant home in a very wonderful neighborhood and presumed it would always be that way.

The house had suffered some fire damage a few years prior to our moving in, but as far as we knew there were no deaths or tragedies of any kind associated with the property. Our home was a two-story white house with a large front yard and an even bigger back one. I always thought that the house looked kind of historic, like it had been around for a while. Still as a child history was normally the farthest thing from my mind and in the end it was just simply a home for us. Needless to say, I never put much thought into it one way or the other.

Before I try to explain how the house came to have a plethora of invisible guests, let me explain my view on the very infamous Ouija boards. I do not think a board of any kind has magical powers. It's my opinion that the Ouija is no more attuned to ghosts than a monopoly board. What brings a ghost instead is the energy that people bring when they try to contact the dead. This can occur with any kind of séance ceremony...the board is just dressing that helps people get their mind in the occult mood. If the person using it is knowledgeable and has the know-how to control the communication between them and the spirit world there is not that much risk; however, if the person is just messing around or just trying to contact anyone, that person can open a door that allows the good, mischievous, or straight-out bad to come though.

So with my personal opinions and feelings on any kind of séance explained I will help you understand how I came to think this way.

In 1988, I was nearly five years old and, as I mentioned earlier, we had been living at our house for about two years. There had been no odd occurrences in the home up to that point. However, soon the wheels were set in motion to change that one summer night.

My oldest sister Lisa had purchased an Ouija board at a toy store in the nearby mall. Being a normal 16-year-old girl, Lisa had bought it just for laughs; neither she nor anyone in the house ever took it seriously. It seemed to be nothing more than a hocus pocus toy, just a step up from the "magic eight ball" made in a factory and sold at toy and department stores. At the most my mom and dad saw it as a waste of good money and my mom didn't like the very idea of it being in her home.

Shortly after buying the Ouija board, Lisa and my brother Michael decided to take it out for a test run and prove it to be a simple and harmless hoax. They absconded candles from the dining room and a lighter from my mom's purse and set the board up in Lisa's room. They arranged everything on top of her old toy box, lit the candles, cut off the lights, and began asking it some questions. Much to their surprise, even from the very beginning, it would seem the board was responding to their questions. Neither of them claimed to be moving the planchette...yet it seemed to be moving. There is no way of knowing how much longer it would have continued because shortly into this my mom walked in on them using it. Being a church-going Baptist she was more than a little bothered by the prospect of them even pretending to talk to the dead, so Michael decided to mess with our mom and move the planchette all around the board just to give the old gal a startle. My mother was not amused and asked them to stop playing with it; Michael and Lisa decided for their own well-being to do as she said, so the Ouija board was packed up. My Mom asked that it be thrown away, but instead the board was put in the hall closet because, after all, it was not free and throwing it away would have been a waste of Lisa's money. Normally, no one would have given it a second thought. The Ouija board should have been forgotten like the other games we had shoved in there over the years, but that was not what would end up happening.

The very first night after it had been used bizarre things began to happen. Nothing big at first... just cold spots that had never been there before and odd thuds and rattling around the house, which were all dismissed easy enough. The cold may have been from a draft in the house and the thuds may have been wood settling. However, it was during the summer, which is an odd time of year for a cold draft that had never been around before to simply start, especially in the South. The thuds also had never accorded before that night.

Very shortly after this whenever anyone was on the second floor they never felt alone. No matter if it was broad daylight or the dark of night, it always felt as if somebody was lurking — someone angry and unseen.

Now of course at the time no one in the house assumed anything paranormal was going on; after all it was just a few cold spots and uneasy feelings, nothing to be alarmed about. However, this compliancy would soon start to change in a hurry.

It was just a few weeks after the Ouija board incident that my mom had the first sign that our new house-guests were there. She and I were home alone; I was playing on the living room floor with some toys and my mom was in the kitchen making us lunch. While she was putting the final touches on my fried bologna sandwich, we heard what sounded like a piece of wood being forcefully rammed against a wall on the second floor hallway.

My mom was afraid it could have been an intruder who had gotten into the house without us knowing. The only staircase to the upstairs was in my sight and I had not seen anything. Additionally, it would have been extremely hard for someone to break in on the second floor of a home in broad daylight. Still it was certain that there was something or someone making this strange noise.

However, the noise abruptly stopped. Silence entombed the house; my mom and I sat waiting to see if any sounds came from the second floor. There was not a follow up sound — no footsteps, voices, or any kind of noise at all that would go along with an unwanted person in the house. My mom decided to investigate despite her fear of who may be up there. She walked up the stairs worried with every step what she might see. I stationed myself at the foot of the steps with my eyes glued to her.

What my mom found baffled her. The wooden hatch in the hallway that led to the attic had been forced open. This shocked my mom, as the attic was too tall to reach without a ladder and there was no ladder to be seen. She was then struck with the even more important question of who had opened it?

My mom was not about to assume it was a "haunt" (her word for a ghost) that was messing with the attic, but she was just not sure what else it could be. My dad was not too worried when he heard about it; he was sure that there was a perfectly good explanation for it. No one was hurt by the incident and that was all that was important to him. Both he and mom put it behind them, assuming this was a one-time event. Little did we know, the strange activity had only started. Very shortly after the attic incident, a large majority of my family would all witness a bizarre and hard-to-explain phenomena.

One evening, my mom was taking Susan, Lisa, Michael, and me to an art crafts store (which she was addicted to her whole life). The only two members who were not in attendance was my dad, who was at work, and my oldest brother Troy, who was out with friends. We were all in the front hall ready to head out when an upstairs light caught my mom's eye. She quickly dispatched Michael to cut off the lights in the upstairs hallway. Michael had just cut off the table lamp right at the top of the staircase and was heading down when to everyone's surprise the light clicked back on! Michael, who was still only halfway down the stairs, simply turned around and cut the lamp back off trying not to think too much about it. He again headed down the stairs and this time he reached the door with the rest of us. As we were about to walk out, the same lamp clicked on once again, but my mom decided to let it be this time.

As my mom told it, she remembered having the distinct feeling that something was toying with her, causing her to feel a little alarmed. She quickly herded the family out the door. We loaded into the station wagon and headed out trying to find something to take the place of the lamp at the top of the stairs in our minds.

After the art store we went out for dinner at a local restaurant. In all we were gone from our house for about two hours. As we drove up to the house, my mom noticed that a lot of the lights were on inside. She just assumed either Troy or my Dad were back. It only took a few moments upon entering the house to realize they weren't, as neither of them responded when she called their names. As we moved from room to room there were even more lights on. Along with the original lamp giving us trouble we found the kitchen light, the bathroom light, and the dining room light on. Apparently one of the ghosts did not like the dark or wanted us to have a really high electric bill.

My parents never really talked about the haunting or ever really referred to it at all with friends or family. They both just accepted it was happening after they ran out of excuses for the odd happenings in our home. After the first few months the ghosts in the house defiantly kept their presence known. They continued to cut on and off the lights, move objects, or make strange noises. However, they had yet to appear to anyone, but that changed late one night for Lisa.

It had been a nice quiet day for everyone and nothing out of the ordinary had taken place. Around two o'clock in the morning my sister Lisa like everyone else in the house was fast asleep. She was never really sure why she woke up, but for some unknown reason she had been compelled to do so. What she saw when she woke up was very startling to her. Lisa said that before she could even focus her eyes she felt like she wasn't alone.

When her eyes adjusted to the darkness, she found herself looking at a row of "faceless nuns" standing by the foot of her bed! Faceless nuns was the best way she felt she could describe them. She saw figures cloaked in black in a way that reminded her of a nun's habit. In the spot that should have been a face was nothing but blackness. They said and did nothing before they quickly disappeared, which left her quite unnerved and confused. Later, she said that despite their somewhat unsettling appearance she was not scared of them and almost felt like they were there to protect her rather than hurt or scare her.

Nevertheless, at the time, Lisa went as fast as she could to wake our parents and tell them what she had seen. My parents assured Lisa that it was most likely a dream and there was nothing to worry about. My mom would much later confess she did not think it was a dream, but did not know what else to tell Lisa at the time that would not scare her. After all, children want parents to protect them and not to be as scared as they are.

The incidents in the house would most often come randomly; it could be days or weeks without so much as a cold spot, and the only constant was the feeling of being watched on the second floor. It was a feeling that did not exist before the Ouija was used, but after its use, the entire family felt it all the time.

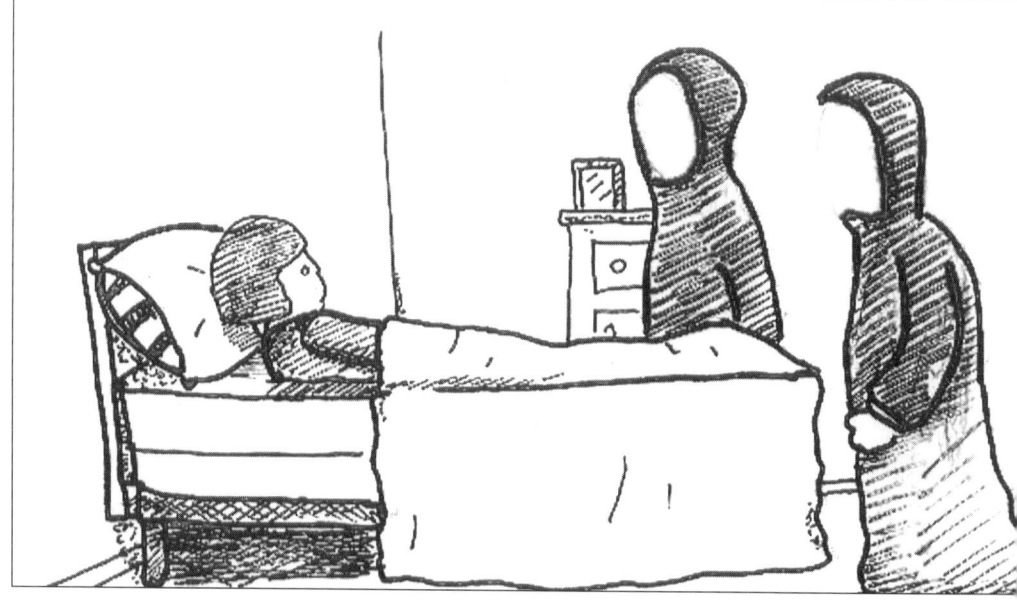

It was on the second floor that I had my first encounter with one of the entities. It was late in the evening during December 1988 and my brother Michael was spending the night with a friend so I was in our room by myself. I was sound asleep until shortly after one in the morning when a loud sound woke me. It took me a moment to figure out what was going on. It was a sound like a very heavy-footed person trudging up the stairs. The footsteps made it up to the top and then began walking down the hallway and past my bedroom. My first thought was that maybe my dad was up or that my brother Troy was coming in late. I peeked out the door and expected to get my answer; instead I didn't see a soul, just a very dark and silent hallway. I slammed the door and darted back to my bed. However, to my surprise the footsteps started again as soon as I was back in bed and walked by my door once again and then seemed to head back down the stairs.

I decided not to take any chances and flung open my door and ran for my parent's room as fast I could. I did not tell my parents exactly what had happened, only that I was scared. They assumed it was simply because I was not used to having a room to myself. I did not really know how to tell them I was scared of footsteps so I let them believe it was as simple as they thought it was. I did not go back to sleep that night.

I wish I could say that was the worst thing that happened to me in the house, but it was nothing compared to the incident that made me a true believer in the paranormal, which happened less than a year later. During the summer of 1989, my mom was downstairs talking to her parents, who had come by for a nice visit (my mom always enjoyed these). I was upstairs playing in my room and feeling comforted by the fact that bright daylight was pouring in through the windows. It was while having this false sense of security that I heard some noises coming from down the hall in my parents' room. It sounded like some boxes were being rummaged through. Assuming that it was either my mom or one of my siblings, I went to check it out, and as I walked towards the room, I heard the noise again. As I entered, I noticed it was coming from their closet so I asked who was in there. I received no response.

Still, I wanted to see who was in there, so I walked toward it. I realized something was wrong when I noticed the closet was about twenty degrees colder than the rest of the room. In my parents' room was a large walk-in closet so I still believed that someone could be in there, hidden by clothes or some boxes. I entered and upon looking around, I still did not see anyone. Then, I had a strong urge to look up toward the ceiling and as soon as I did I received the most profound paranormal experience of my life. My mom's closet had an attic access hatch like the one in the hallway... it was fully open and staring down at me were two hideous faces! They were not some stereotypical ghosts. They did not appear see-through but as fully solid beings and they did not disappear before my eyes. These two beings stared at me with their black empty sockets. They seemed to be moving their heads in a mocking way and they were defiantly laughing and enjoying the fear they were causing me.

Two eerie spirits gaze down from the attic.

I was frozen for only a second or two and then I ran out of my parents' room and raced down the stairs so fast it is a wonder I did not trip and break my neck. My first thought was not about ghosts, but that one of my siblings was playing a prank on me. Being the youngest of five, I was often fair game. At the time I really knew almost nothing about ghosts and based what little I knew on Halloween and "Casper" cartoons.

As far as I knew, ghosts had on white sheets and were see-through and looked nothing like what I saw that day. So when I got to the bottom of the stairs and ran up to my mom I was a little shocked that all my siblings were accounted for and talking with my grandparents. I tried to explain what happened, but my mom, not wanting her parents to think we were crazy, kept acting like I had imagined it and made it clear that it was not a good time to be talking about such things. I spent the rest of the day downstairs and did not dare go back upstairs until the rest of the family was up there; for some reason their presence made me feel a little safer.

When I was starting on this book and getting my mom's account of things, she let me know she believed me. Wanting to see if anything was in the closet, she had gone to check out what I had told her later that very day. She told me that she was shocked to find the attic hatch was open. She felt that this was odd because nobody ever went up there and the only people tall enough to open it were either not home at the time or had been downstairs with her. She never told me when I was young about this because she was not sure how to explain it to me and, as time went by, it had faded from her mind.

We had multiple entities in our house. The one in the attic was pretty mean, the nuns in my sister's room seemed protective, and the phantom guy walking in the hallway was noisy, but, as it turned out, there was one more entity in the house. My mom was sure she was, in fact, helped by the protective entities in the house late one evening in 1989. She was sound asleep in her room and she had a very vivid dream. In the dream there was a house much like ours on fire. People were jumping from the window on fire and screaming in terror. It horrified her so bad she awoke in a cold sweat. She figured despite how real it seemed it was just a dream and headed downstairs to brew some tea. She would always drink iced tea to help her calm down.

As she reached the bottom of the stairs, mom noticed a faint burning smell. Not sure what to make of it, she headed toward the kitchen. She looked around the kitchen to see if anything had been left on or was burning, but found nothing. She put it out of her mind and began brewing some tea.

As she was waiting for the water to boil, she noticed my dad had fallen asleep on the couch in the living room watching TV. She went over to cut off the television and wake my dad. It was then that she noticed smoke coming from the blanket my dad was using. She soon discovered that he had fallen asleep with a lit cigarette in his hand. She acted quickly and doused the small fire with a glass of water, which of course woke my dad and after some explaining he thanked her and apologized for what could have started a horrible fire. My mom admitted that, at the time, she did not really connect the dream with what almost happened and merely thought we were real lucky she woke up when she did.

Like most bizarre events in the house, my mom never talked about it until many years later, when she felt less likely that she would be thought to be crazy. She told me, only within the last year of her life, about that one truly good thing that the ghost seemed to do for our family. It would seem that at least one of our guests did not wish to see my family harmed.

My family moved out of Sunset the summer of 1989. It was not because of issues with the paranormal, but the fact that Lisa was moving out and Troy was going off to college, it seemed a smaller place would make more financial sense. At that point, my mom was still acting like she did not believe the house was haunted, but all of us noticed the moment she found the Ouija board in the closet and made sure it was thrown away...deep below the garbage.

My mom, Susan, and I would, many years later, live through another haunted house. After our second go-round in the land of the haunted, my mom became more willing to discuss the events at Sunset once she realized it was nothing to be ashamed of. I often talked to her about it when she came to visit Michael and me, but I did not interview her about it until a few months before she passed on. I had the chance to get her whole account and her thoughts on it and I am glad I have her take on what happened all those years ago.

Chapter One

The Mountains

Samuel Reed House

If you want grandeur mixed with a quaint mountain setting, you could not ask for a better place to stay than the Samuel Reed House Bed and Breakfast in Asheville. The design of the historic home will no doubt amaze and astound anyone who looks upon it. The imposing house was built over a hundred years ago in 1892. Samuel Harrison Reed had this impressive house built for him and his family; the location for his family home had less to do with the view, which brings people there today, and more to with his job. Samuel was a successful lawyer in his time and one of his biggest clients was the extremely rich and powerful George Vanderbilt. Samuel's new home was built within eyesight of the Vanderbilt mansion, which made him more accessible to his client. If you have never seen or heard of the Vanderbilt mansion, the best way to describe it would be to say that the White House would be just the right size to be its tool shed. It is an extremely large structure.

The Reed House is a two-story, pale yellow mansion with ten rooms and two wings. It sits on the top of a low mountain, which gives it a breathtaking view of the nearby landscape. Within its walls are five guest rooms, a library, game room, family room, and even a secret passageway that, of course, no home should be without. No doubt, the Reed family had a comfortable life while they resided there. Sure they did not have the massiveness of the Vanderbilts, but they were still better off than most people of their time.

Samuel Reed was born to Joseph and Katherine Reed in 1851. An ambitious young man Samuel received his law degree from the University of North Carolina in 1872 and married his wife Jessie Wingate just one year later. Samuel was determined to make his mark in the world; he soon began his law career at which he would excel in.

He was a senior member of the law firm Reed and Van Winkle by the time construction on his family home had started, which was no small task by any measure. With his success as a lawyer, Reed and his wife tried to start a family; they did, in fact, eventually succeed in giving birth to nine children, but, sadly, only four lived beyond infancy. Their home was a place of joy most of the time, but the family would suffer more loss as they lived there. In 1905, Samuel's wife passed away; he followed suit six month later, leaving their twelve-year-old son, Wingate Reed, with the house.

After going off to school and marrying, Wingate finally moved into the house in 1913, but after only a year he decided it was much too large for his needs and sold it to the first of what would be many new owners. The house passed hands many times over the following decades and eventually ended up in the hands of AKM Abbot in 1964. Abbot divided the house into multiple apartments that he then rented while he continued to own the property.

It was at this time, as the Reed house served as a home to multiple families, that one of the first ghost encounters took place there. In the 1970s a small family we will call the Smiths had moved into one of the apartments in the Reed house, a husband and wife along with several teenage children. No doubt they were very happy with their new home and the natural beauty that came with it. It is safe to say that like most families a "ghost" being in the home never crossed any of their minds, but they would soon find out their new home had some of its former residents still lurking around.

They did not have to wait long at all to meet these phantom housemates. It all started on their very first night in their new home, as Mrs. Smith awoke to the sound of loud footsteps coming up the back of the old servant's stairs. Her mind was racing to figure out what she was hearing. She first checked to make sure all her children were where they should be, asleep in their rooms, and sure enough she found all her little ones in their beds. Her second thought was to make sure no one who was not supposed to be there had gotten into her new home. She nervously checked the stairs and hallways, but each one was empty. In the meantime the sound had stopped. She never found an answer to the strangeness inside the apartment.

However, this would turn out not to be a one-time phenomenon because for the rest of the time they lived in the home the footsteps would seem to return every few nights. The family eventually had the stairs carpeted hoping that would put an end to the footsteps; instead they simply became softer, but they still could be heard every few nights like before.

It was during their first Christmas in their new home when the family was hosting a party. Mrs. Smith was telling her guest about the paranormal phenomenon the family had encountered while living there. This got a big laugh from a largely skeptical party guest who looked at it as nothing more than campfire ghost stories. While the guest continued having his or her fun, without warning, the family's firmly planted Christmas tree slammed to the ground with amazing speed. Everyone stopped their laughing and was left speechless staring at the toppled tree and broken ornaments all over the floor. Even though no one directly blamed the ghosts that evening, no one else laughed at them either, not wishing to see what they would do next if furthered provoked, It would appear that the invisible house-guest does not like being laughed at.

One of the still continuing odd happenings in the home takes place in the game room involving the timeless game of pool. Most people enjoy a good game of pool now and then, I know I do, even the deceased it would seem like to have a game as well. For many years the sounds of a pool game have been heard in the empty room, the noise of clacking balls and faint talking have been reported by guest and visitors coming from the game room, sometimes so loud people about to enter the room are convinced they are about to walk in on a game only to find the room going dead silent and completely empty as they enter.

It is not always just the sound coming from the table, but an actual game sometimes seems to have been in the process of being played, folks have come in and find what should be a perfectly racked up set of billiard balls only to find them scattered across the table as if they are in the middle of a game. Most think that this is none other than Samuel Reed himself, he was known to like a good game of in his earthly days. Maybe Samuel is just trying to get a few games in while no one is looking, as for who his partner in this game is, no one is sure about that one.

The house stopped functioning as an apartment building and fell into deep neglect as it waited for someone new to take ownership. The extremely poor condition of the historic house soon threatened to have the former beautiful home condemned by the city of Ashville.

Luckily in 1973 Marguerite Turcot purchased the house and land; she then began the hard work of restoring the home to its original glory that Samuel had constructed all those decades ago. She would not finish all the renovations herself, however, because the house was sold to Hotch and Owen Sullivan in 2000 and they finished restoring it, making it once again a beautiful addition to Asheville as the Biltmore Wingate Inn.

It should be a testament to the grandeur and beauty of the house that even something like death cannot keep its former owners away. They still like to hang around and play a game of pool, or possibly just knock over a Christmas tree to let folks know they are still around.

Battery Park Hotel

Battery Park Hotel, one of Asheville's treasures, was known for class and elegance. It has stood proudly for over a hundred years, although it has changed quite a bit during its existence.

In actuality, the hotel had two lives; originally it was built in 1886 by a man named Colonel Frank Cox who desired to build a top of the line establishment in the mountain community. The Hotel was ahead of its time with amenities such as electricity and elevators long before those types of things were readily available. For nearly four decades, it was well known and looked at as a source of pride by the people of Asheville.

In the early 1920s, Edwin W. Grove purchased an already somewhat aged hotel, he was ready to make some big changes to it but instead of renovating or touching it up he simply had it torn down! At the time this was not very popular with many of the local residents, but Mr. Grove reason to destroy it was to build a more modern and even more luxuries hotel then the original.

In 1924, the new Battery Park Hotel opened; built with neoclassical and Spanish romanticism architecture, it had over two hundred rooms available for those who traveled to the mountain town and needed a place to prop their feet up in style.

The hotel would remain open until 1972 and, in those forty-eight years of business, staff and guests alike created a lot of good memories, along with some not so happy ones. It can certainly be said that any location with history to it is going have some tragic and unfortunate events attached to it on some level.

Among such occurrences that have reportedly taken place, there were claims that a few folks may have taken advantage of building's roof, not for star gazing or a view of the landscape, but, instead, to sadly end their lives by jumping to their death on more than one occasion. Some of those poor souls have been seen reliving those last tragic moments of their life. People who go by the former hotel will, now and then, see, what they believe, a living person jump from the roof of the former hotel. Acting quickly and with compassion, as one would expect in given situations, they will call the authorities, hoping that somehow they can save these people. No bodies are ever found and there are no signs that anyone had jumped. The emotional traumas that led those people up there in life seems to keep some part of them there in death as well.

Other deaths linked to the location where not self inflected but the acts of a deranged one. On July 17, 1936, the body of Helen Clevenger was discovered in Room 224, which she was residing in at the time. She was a young beauty, seemingly without an enemy in the world, which made the horrific nature of her demise even more troubling; it was a particularly savage one that involved a beating, slashing with a knife and finally a gun shot. With the surrounding community in shock, a large-scale investigation was set into motion to track down the perpetrator of this brutal crime.

Her murderer was eventually brought to justice. He was one of the hotel's employees whose name was Martin Moore. Confessing to the heinous crime, Moore stated that he had found himself attracted to the young Ms. Clevenger and apparently tried to force himself on her, an act that resulted in her untimely demise. He was found guilty and sentenced to death, meeting his end via the gas chamber.

Often people believe that murder victims only haunt a location until their killers are brought to justice but it would seem this is not true in Helen's case; her apparition was often seen in the hotel wondering the halls in a daze long after Moore was executed. She has often given people quite a fright, since she is described as a transparent, almost mist like, form of a human that simply floats down the hall and pays no mind to those she scares.

Her apparition was not the only thing she was known for. Often guests and employees would feel like they were being watched by invisible eyes around the hotel and odd noises could be heard from empty rooms, including the sound of furniture being moved around when none had and phantom thuds on the wall were some of the incidents.

Helen is thought to be the cause of disembodied crying that was heard throughout the hotel, but most often could be heard in her old room. Others who stayed in Room 224 would feel a heavy sadness permeating through the air while they were in there. Strong cold spots would appear in random pockets of the room and there would be the uncomfortable feeling of being watched by an unseen force as they tried to sleep.

Even though the building stopped functioning as a hotel in 1972, it does not sit as another vacant building. In the 1980s, it was purchased by the Asheville Housing Authority, which has since turned it into a set of apartment buildings. Some phantoms continue to be seen in the former hotel's grand halls to this day, but seem to cause none of the newer residents too much trouble.

Smith McDowell House

I have already named many of Asheville's historic treasures, but there are so many more. The famous American novelist Thomas Wolfe called Asheville home; now his mothers' old boarding house is a museum dedicated to him. Not a fan of literature? You could visit the very renowned Baltimore estate, which of course I have already mentioned.

All the countless historic locations of Asheville are wonderful places to visit, but I am going to be talking about a certain location in this mountain town — the Smith McDowell House. It is the oldest brick residence in Asheville, an antebellum home constructed around twenty years before the Civil War started. The four-story home is built on a land grant given to a colonel from the American Revolution, Daniel Smith.

It was not Daniel Smith who would end up building the famous home on the site, but his son James McConnell (1787-1856). James was reported to be the first child of European parents born west of the Blue Ridge Mountains. As an adult James would marry Mary "Polly" Patton (1794-1853), who was his loving and loyal partner the rest of her life. James was not just a local resident of Asheville, but an all-around Renaissance man in the world of business. He ran a state licensed toll bridge over the French broad river at the Buncombe's turnpike; this being a vital route for farmers to trade made sure James McConnell turned a tidy profit. Still he did so much more then run a toll bridge. Among other things, he owned a gold mine, a store, the Buck Hotel, two plantations, a Tavern, and a tannery. With all this financial success came some political gains also: James McConnell served as mayor of Asheville and a Judge during his life.

With a fortune and his wife by his side James used his father's land to build a home for them. The house we now know as the Smith McDowell House would be a labor of love for James. There are no records of the house's construction so a lot of what is known is based on educated guesses. The detailed construction of the house certainly suggests a skilled architect was used and Mr. Smith owned over forty slaves who most likely were also used during construction as labor. The brick that was used was very possibly made in Asheville itself; where clay perfect for brick-making was abundant and would have been significantly less expensive than shipping from other locations in the state. When it was finished James and his family proudly called it their home.

The house would eventually pass to his son, John Patton Smith, in 1856. John would only live in the house for a year because in 1857 he joined his father in death; not really a lot of time to enjoy his inheritance. Next the house landed in the hands of a business partner and son-in-law of James McConnell, William Wallace McDowell (there is the McDowell part of the house's name).

Soon after the house fell into McDowell's possession, the Civil War started and he being a proud southerner would leave his new home and family to serve in the Confederate army. Like many other southerners the McDowells suffered economic downturn after the war was over. Their finances got so bad that in 1881 the McDowells sold their home to an Irish immigrant by the name of Alexander Garrett, who became the first of many owners to do remodeling work on the house. Although they were not major changes, his construction on the house helped give it the layout it still has to this day.

The home went through a slew of owners in the next hundred years, which included millionaires, friends of President Theodore Roosevelt, and even the Catholic Diocese, to name just a few. In 1974, it was purchased by its current owners, Asheville-Buncombe's Technical Community College. At this point the historic antebellum home had become dilapidated and would have to undergo extensive restoration. The site was added to the National Register of Historic places, and in 1981, the nonprofit Smith McDowell Museum opened to the public.

The outside of the home is still very much like it would have been in the 1840s, with the exception of the carriage house, which was not added until 1898. As for the inside of the historic site, some of its antebellum style is there, but the majority of the home is a product of a major remodeling that started in 1913 while the house belonged to Brewster Chapman. Brewster did the most extensive renovations of any of the house's owners, drastically changing the interior of the home from its original look.

The home is well cared for now; this wonderful historic site is a place of loving preservation that is maintained by a staff that strives to keep history alive for today's and tomorrow's generation. Perhaps all this TLC is the reason some of the home's former inhabitants have apparently stuck around after they punched the clock of life so to speak — they still see it as their home.

It has been reported that the house is home to disembodied voices, phantom footsteps, and odd lights that seem to appear and then vanish with no explanation. The haunting at the house goes as far back as the museum does and possibly even farther; after all, who knows what the past owners may have seen or heard and simply decided to keep to themselves?

Sarah Harrison is no stranger to the world of the paranormal; she is herself a member of a paranormal investigation team and even worked on a paranormal themed show called "Another Dimension." It was while working on the show that she was brought to the Smith McDowell House. Sarah was performing her duties as a camera operator for the show that morning, and she and the rest of the show's crew, along with a local news team, had arrived at the site before the house's staff. The home was still locked tight as a drum from the night before. Sarah knew this as a fact for she tried to enter the front door and found it locked. With no way in, she decided to wait in the backyard for the staff to show up. It was while sitting there that Sarah was startled when the back door opened unexpectedly. No, it was not a ghost, but the news crew that was joining them, which had somehow entered the house.

Sarah asked the folks from the news crew if the house staff had arrived and she just didn't notice. The answer surprised her: she was informed that the house staff had not arrived and the door — the very one Sarah had tried — was just unlocked! Additionally, the news crew informed Sarah that while in the house they could hear music, but were unable to figure out where it was coming from. The news crew agreed that the music was definitely not from this era. Upon hearing it they simply assumed it was some kind of record being played to help create the atmosphere in the house.

Sarah went back around the house to check and see the unlocked door for herself; however, when she got there it was locked tight as a tick...just as it had been before. No matter how she fiddled with the knob to make sure it could not be forced open, it stayed locked; there was no two ways about it!

When the Smith McDowell's house staff arrived, they were as baffled as anyone. They were also at a complete loss to explain the music that had been heard. None of the records in the house duplicated the music reported or would have been on when the house was empty. Stranger still was the burning question: why would the ghost let the news crew in and not Sarah? Sarah said she did not take it personally.

Lisa Whitfield is the education director of the Smith McDowell House Museum and has been working there for a number of years. She has witnessed a handful of unexplainable or just plain odd moments while performing her duties. Lisa seems to be a very level-headed woman who is not one to claim "ghost" at the first phantom thud. From her various encounters, she has come to believe that there are several ghosts residing in the historic site.

In early 2006 Lisa and the rest of the staff were kind enough to honor a mother's request of a birthday gift for her son turning ten. Her son was a fan of ghost-hunting and the paranormal in general, and Lisa had arranged for him to do a private investigation at the Smith McDowell House. Lisa was on hand to supervise that day and make sure all necessary precautions were taken to ensure the safety of the boy and the house.

The young investigator took photos and tried recording EVPs. Nothing extraordinary happened, but when he brought out a small ball that would change. He was on the third floor of the house near the staircase. The boy had with him a small ball he had brought to "provoke" one of the spirits. He let whatever spirits that might be there know he was going to be rolling the ball on the floor and if any of them would like to roll it back he would much appreciate it.

Lisa admitted she was not really expecting to see anything from this experiment. She watched the boy roll the ball, putting some good force behind it. Lisa was shocked when the ball continued full speed across the room only to stop dead in its tracks! As if the ball's sudden stop wasn't alarming enough, next it rapidly rolled back to the boy, as if a hand pushed it.

Lisa, the boy, and his mother were at a loss for words. Oddly the ball kept rolling, passing the boy and heading toward the stairs. The ball hit the first stair with a high bounce, and then proceeded to land on the next one and the one right after that! The ball didn't miss a single step on its journey to the bottom and it never moved from the center of each step. It finally stopped dead in its tracks on the very last stair! The fact the ball continued down the stairs without slowing down one bit yet the second it reached the very last step it just ceased was beyond weird for all those who were there. The rest of the young man's investigation was without incident. Regardless it was a birthday he will no doubt remember. The boy felt extremely fortunate, seeing how some people can go years doing investigations and never have anything like this happen. No doubt he must of felt like he had hit the paranormal lottery.

To share a paranormal moment with other people can be very comforting, as you know that your mind and eyes are not playing tricks on you. Generally experiencing one by yourself normally is enough to make you want to pack it in and call it a day. Lisa was alone one day when one of the house's residents showed up for a visit and even called her by name.

She was in her office, which is located on the third floor of the house, doing some paperwork. She was one of only two people in the house at the time, the other being a male volunteer on the first floor. Lisa was burying herself in her job at hand and enjoying the solitude when she distinctly heard a male voice call her name. She said it sounded as if it were coming from the nearby staircase. She got up from her desk and expected to see the volunteer waiting for her with some question or problem; instead Lisa saw a completely empty staircase. Lisa went and found the volunteer and asked him if he had called her. He said he hadn't and had been working nowhere near her office. She, needless to say, was tossed for a jolt. If the only other living person in the building had not called her, it only left the ethereal ones. Lisa accepted it for what it was and continued her work. For the rest of the day Lisa was left wondering what the disembodied person wanted with her in the first place.

Visitors and volunteers alike have reported many phenomena occurring over the years. Lisa is not the only person to hear phantom voices within the house's walls. Visitors have also reported seeing full-bodied apparitions generally of a man staring through one of the upstairs windows. The real question is why these various spirits have chosen to stick around the home. It is very likely that so many of its former owners had such a devotion to it in life they feel compelled to stick around after death.

The museum is open to the public year-round, bringing parts of North Carolina's past back to life for those who care to learn more about it. It allows visitors to see rooms and furnishings that are from another time, which can easily whisk visitors to another era in American history. With such a preserved historical site, it is not hard to imagine that those that may have lived there in the past still could be confused into thinking they still do.

Grove Park Inn

If you ever found yourself on Sunset Mountain in Western North Carolina, do not be shocked if you see a hotel that suddenly seems to just come out of the mountain. It is not a trick of the mind, but is in fact the Grove Park Inn, which was designed to match the surrounding granite rock in the mountain to make it seem as if it is actually a part of the mountain itself. The Grove Park Inn is a testament to the unique desire of one man, his unwillingness to shake from his vision, and the longevity of his structure that belongs to the ages.

In 1912, an owner of a pharmaceutical company Edwin Wiley Grove had purchased a patch of land on Sunset Mountain with a simple desire to construct an inn, which would match his own design. His design was unlike other contemporary hotels of his time (or any time for that matter). He did not care about the cost or even the challenges of building his vision; he just knew he wanted it done!

Edwin was determined to stay true to what he envisioned. He went through many local architects, but none of them could grasp what he wanted and most tried to twist his design to fit theirs. Edwin kept trying, unwilling to compromise no matter what people told him. He looked until he found a man who would give him his mountain hotel. He eventually found the right person in the form of his own son-in-law, Fred L. Sealy. The vision he fought so strongly to bring to life was one of a hotel that would not just be built on the mountain, but would also look as if it was actually a part of it.

Edwin was determined that the hotel would be constructed from the same type of rock as the mountain, which was granite. In addition to this, the stones they used had to have only the sun side — worn and naturally aged — facing outward, for the world to see, to truly give it the desired feel of being part of the mountain.

Once off the ground, work progressed at lightning pace. Amazingly it took just under a year from its beginning for the entire project to be finished and, in 1913, Grove Park Inn was opened to the general public. The Inn consisted of five sections that joined end to end, making it an impressive structure not only in design but size as well.

After the doors were opened, the hotel never seemed to have any trouble keeping its rooms full of guests who desired to stay in a one-of-a-kind hotel. The design's uniqueness, along with the wondrous view it provided, made sure it was a success. Over the years, the number of celebrities and powerful guests who have stayed there could fill a book of its own; among them were Thomas Edison, President Woodrow Wilson, and John D. Rockefeller.

During World War II, the Inn was taken over by the United States Military and used as a detainment camp for Axis diplomats. It also functioned as a base of government for the Philippine exiled leaders, who resided in the presidential cottage, while their lands were occupied by the Imperial Japanese forces. Needless to say, not every hotel can boast that kind of guest list.

All and all these are rather amazing facts about the Inn, but some would say it pales in comparison to what many folks know the Grove Park Inn best for. The Inn's most famous guest of all is not a president or a star of the silver screen, but someone known, simply, as The Pink Lady.

No one can say what her real name was or who she was in life. All that seems to be known for sure is that she was a guest at the inn in 1920. She had been staying in Room 545, which is on the Palm Court located on the fifth floor of the hotel. One evening, tragedy befell her and she lost her life. It is unclear whether she was pushed or if she jumped of her own accord; there are many people who believe either story. Whatever the reasons and methods were, general consensus is that she fell to her death at the Palm Court of the Grove Park Inn and everyone agrees that she was wearing a pink dress at the time.

The Pink Lady's five-story fall should have been the end of her. As it turned out, this was just the beginning of her story. Shortly after her death, the first reports of sightings of a phantom woman in pink in the halls emerged — most of them occurring in or near Room 545.

Witnesses of her presence would often describe seeing an average looking woman who was dressed in a pink gown. She is reported to leave a cold chill in her wake and then, simply, vanish without a trace, leaving behind confused witnesses. The Pink Lady does not seem to be very shy; in fact she has been seen so frequently since her death that the hotel's management just accepts her as a harmless and permanent addition to the hotel. It is not a stretch to say the hotel is a little proud of their Pink Lady, who does not spread fear; rather, she is often enjoyed by those who encounter her.

The Pink Lady is no one trick pony; she does not always show up as a full-bodied apparition. Some people who encounter her report only seeing a mist flying down the hall. Often, the mist is described as pink in hue (just like her dress). At other times, people are tapped on the shoulder from an invisible person. Some have even heard a voice whispering near them and though it is normally too low for them to understand what is being said, it is quite clearly a woman's voice.

In the 1950s, a painter was working in Room 545. Initially, it did not even cross his mind that the room was of any special interest. After he entered the room and started to paint, he immediately felt a cold chill. Of course, there were other more reasonable explanations than the chill being caused by a ghost, so he brushed it off. He tried to get on with his work, but the cold chill would not leave and it was soon accompanied by a very strong feeling of uneasiness. He felt as if someone's eyes were watching his every move. Before very long, he decided that enough was enough and left the room quickly, refusing to finish his painting duties in there.

The painter had not experienced anything like it in any of the other rooms he had worked in before. For him, Room 545 was like no other; the peculiar events within that room provided a singular event for sure! It would seem that the Pink Lady did not like him painting *her* room; however, this was not the first time a spirit had shown disapproval with a change to their environment, though displeasure is rarely shown while work is actually being done.

Over the decades, some employees and guests have gotten more than just an odd feeling — they have actually been physically touched by the famous lady! One guest, Kathy J. Urban, was staying with her husband on the fifth floor. One night, they were both sound asleep when Kathy awoke to loud noises coming from the hall. She assumed that it was someone checking into the next room. While trying to tune it out and go back to sleep, she felt someone holding her hand. Her first thought was that it was her husband, but that changed when she realized he was positioned on the wrong side, so it was impossible that he was holding that hand! Fearfully, she opened her eyes to see who was in the room with them. She looked around the darkened room, but no one was there. In addition, there were no signs that anyone had entered or exited the room while they slept. Yet her hand was still tingling...as if someone had

Brown Mountain Lights 31

just let go. The next day, while talking to a desk clerk, she was informed that no one had checked into any of the rooms on the fifth floor nor had any of the employees been called to the floor during the night.

Many new employees of the Grove Park Inn will see a woman in pink enter a room, bathroom, or turn a corner, but just as surely as the phantom lady appears, she vanishes or dissipates into a mist before their eyes. Whenever this phenomenon is reported to others who are familiar with this peculiar event, they are simply told, "That's just the Pink Lady... get used to her." She has never been anything but a welcomed guest at the Inn and she has never harmed or threatened anyone during her extended stay. In fact, seeing her — or at least encountering her presence in some way — is a goal of many people. Thus, generations of Pink Lady groupies are created and the fifth floor is the place to be when visiting the Grove Park Inn if you hope to join that club.

Brown Mountain Lights

Located in the foothills of the Blue Ridge Mountains in western North Carolina is one of the Tar Heel State's oldest phenomenon: the Brown Mountain Lights. These phantom lights have been seen by countless people for hundreds of years and appear differently to those who see them. Some people have reported seeing them as stationary balls of light or fast-moving blurs while others claim to have seen them disappear and reappear all along the mountain. Regardless of how they appear, everyone agrees they are seeing something they cannot quite explain, although there have been many attempts to do so.

The First European to see the ghostly lights was a German engineer by the name of Geraud de Brahm, who was exploring the mountains in the year 1771. He recorded the sighting in his journal; his writings revealed that he was truly baffled by the sight. The lights looked like nothing he had ever witnessed. As people continued to settle into this region over the following decades, more sightings were reported and soon possible causes were being cultivated by the locals to help explain what was being seen.

One of the first explanations that came from denizens of the fledgling Carolinian state was that the lights revolved around the story of a hunter who went on the mountain one day to bring in some deer and disappeared without a trace. Legend has it that one of his slaves was sent to find him. The servant began wandering the mountain with a lantern looking for his master, traveling from one end to the other. He was never able to find him and the legend goes that he still carries around a lantern on the mountain, still searching, determined to find his former master.

Another even better known story for the famous lights revolves around a poor abused wife who met a sad end on the mountain at the hands of her abusive husband. In the 1850s, a husband and wife lived on Brown Mountain. The wife was very well liked by the community and known to be a pleasant woman; her husband was not nearly as highly regarded and it is believed that he was cheating on her. He was a drunkard and violent man who was strongly disliked by anyone who ever met him, save for the possible exception of his girlfriend with whom he cheated on his wife.

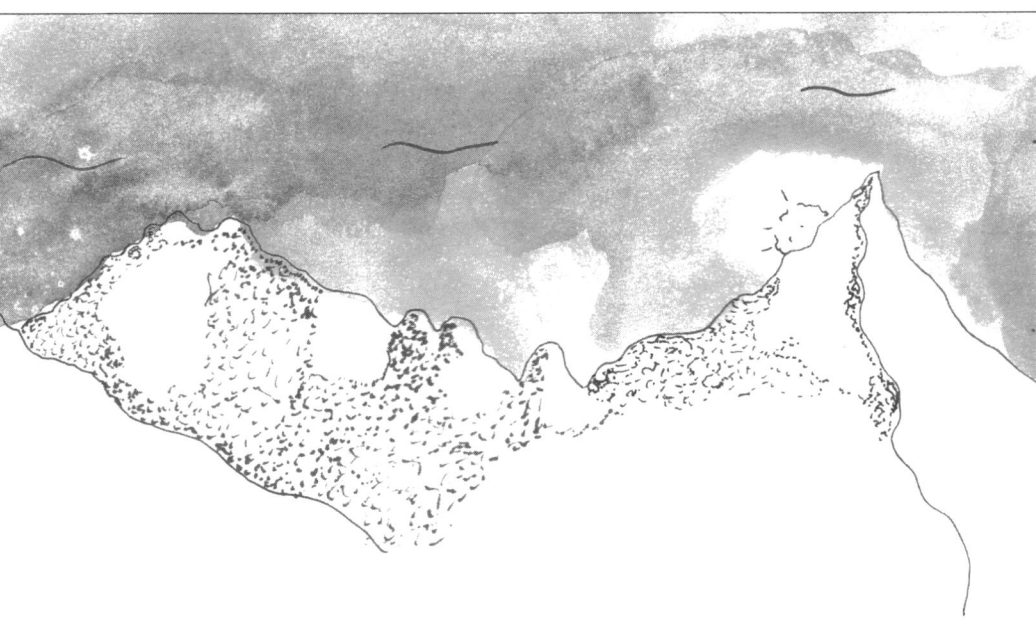

The wife had told a few of her close friends that she believed she was pregnant and she had hoped the news would help heal her troubled marriage; however, it would not. Soon she disappeared, but, due to her popularity in the small community, it did not take much time for the locals to notice her absence. Her husband was quick to tell curious people that his wife had moved back with her family, but would give no further information. Additionally, he would become extremely aggressive to those who attempted to find out more. No one really believed him and his explanations; due to their awareness of his violent streak, the worst was assumed. Even though her husband insisted that she was alive and well, the townsfolk began a search for her body. Naturally, this search angered the husband greatly. Is it possible that he feared that they would uncover something that he did not wish to become public? Shortly after this, he fled and was never seen or heard from again.

Search parties combed the mountain day and night; many of them reported seeing the ghostly lights. Many believed the lights could have been her ghost trying to lead them to her corpse, but her remains were never discovered. It wouldn't be until shortly after the Civil War ended that skeletal remains were found by a group of hunters at the bottom of a chasm on the mountain. After medical examination it was identified as the remains of a young woman. There was little doubt in most people's minds whose bones they were.

Despite the interesting nature of these two stories, neither of these stories can actually be the origin of the lights themselves. The Cherokee tribes witnessed these lights as early as 1200. They, as the Europeans and Americans did, believe that restless spirits caused the lights. The Cherokee tell of a great battle with the Catawba, where many braves died. Some stories say the lights are of those of the tribe's women who went looking for their husbands and sons. Some people also believe that it is the braves who died during the battle that still linger on the mountain and are possibly reliving the battle that took their lives.

Other non-paranormal explanations have been put forth as well, but none of them seem to stick. Everything from train lights and car headlights have been suggested as possible reasons. Of course, you would then have to dismiss the fact that the lights existed hundreds of years before both forms of transportation. Others have said it is swamp lights, which is caused by the gases that naturally occur in marsh and swamps, but Brown Mountain has neither swamps nor marshes on or near the mountain.

Whatever the cause, the lights are not as common as some would believe. Often they do not appear for weeks at a time, and with no guarantee at how long they will last when they do show up. Still when they show up they can be seen from far distances by anyone looking toward the mountains.

The lights are not the only phenomenon that has been reported on the mountain... Some have seen full-bodied apparitions while on the mountain as well.

A young man by the name of Christopher Hutchins, a lifetime resident of North Carolina, shared with me an encounter that happened to him while on a hunting trip on Brown Mountain. Late one evening in 1980, Chris was out with his father and his hunting buddy when they stopped the truck somewhere on the mountain where they hoped some deer would be. While his father and his friend went to check for possible game, Chris, who had decided that he had done enough walking for one day, was waiting in the truck. As he waited, the Carolina sky got continuously darker.

Chris spent most of the time just looking out the window, which led to him eventually noticing a white light slowly moving down the road toward him. At first, Chris did not pay much attention to it, thinking it was nothing more than another car coming down the road, but then he started to notice how slow it was moving, and realized it was only one large light instead of two headlights. As it came closer, he noticed something that made him break into a cold sweat and freeze in fear.

The light was in the shape of a human — a woman to be more precise! As it walked closer, Chris got a better look at it. She was transparent and wore a white dress; in addition to this, she seemed to have dark hair and appeared to be around the age of 20. It was difficult for him to clearly see her face even though she was only a few feet away from him. The ghostly woman never paid Chris any attention. She just continued looking forward as she walked; even as she walked right through the front of Chris's dad's truck she seemed oblivious to him. After walking through the truck, she continued her march down the road and faded in the distance.

It was some time before Chris's dad and his friend made it back to the truck. It did not take his father too long to realize something was wrong with Chris, who sat silently as his face remained ashen with shock. As they began the drive home, his dad asked what happened and Chris told him. His father believed him fully and even suggested that the apparition may have been the ghost of a local girl who had vanished some years before and was thought to have been killed by a cult.

Another option is that it may be the ghost of the poor wife who was killed by her husband in the 1850s. In any case Chris is positive of what he saw that night...a ghostly girl who seemed to be stuck on the mountain for some reason, making a silent march up the road.

As for the lights that have made the mountain so famous, what is known is the Brown Mountain Lights do, in fact, exist. Though some folks say that the lights are ghosts and others choose a more natural explanation, the Brown Mountain Lights are eternally attached to North Carolina folklore and history. And that, mind you, is the way it always should be.

1927 Lake Lure Inn

The historic 1927 Lake Lure Inn located on the Blue Ridge Mountain was, as the name would suggest, opened in 1927 after only taking about one year to construct. Those who visit the Inn note a rather distinct charm emanating from its pale yellow stucco exterior, which seems to match the peaceful surroundings. Upon entering the establishment, guests are greeted by a very large main foyer that is filled with many interesting antiques that send the lucky viewers on an almost spiritual journey back to the era when the Inn was first opened.

The Inn was the brainchild of Dr. Lucius Morse. He fell in love with the surrounding landscape and envisioned a gorgeous lakeside community and resort. At the time, the only problem he faced was that there wasn't a Lake Lure to build his community around! This did not stop Lucius because after 1925, when he had the nearby Rocky River dammed, Lake Lure was born, which, in turn, paved the way for the Inn itself. The name came from his wife Elizabeth Parkenson, who was convinced that people would be drawn or *lured* to the lake, but the envisioned grand resort that was supposed to grow from this small beginning would never come to be.

The Great Depression began in 1929, making such spending highly impractical; the average American was unlikely to go to a lake resort when they could not pay the rent or feed their families. Despite this challenge, the Inn survived the Depression and has become a beloved piece of North Carolina's heritage. Over the years, many have turned it into a wonderful vacation destination.

Like many large scale inns with a few decades of history behind it, more than a few notable characters have spent a night or two at Lake Lure Inn, including Presidents Calvin Coolidge and Franklin D. Roosevelt, our commander through the worst of the Great Depression and World War II.

However, many average, everyday citizens, who fell for the beauty of Lake Lure, have also spent a night or two in the beautiful inn. Countless folks who leave their own personal marks on the inn have been coming and going for over eighty years now.

Over the last few years, the inn's staff has become convinced that some of its former guests have decided to stay as permanent residents, even after they've departed from their mortal coils. In recent years, spectral guests have started making their presence known to random folks around the Inn.

The most famous specter is supposed to haunt Room 215. Legend states she was a young woman killed by her boyfriend sometime during the 1930s after he saw her flirting with another man. The story goes that, in an act of pure jealousy and anger, he killed her. Despite the little that anyone knows about her, it is most commonly accepted that she is the ghost.

One former housekeeper reported many odd encounters in Room 215. When she would clean it, the housekeeper would find long black hairs on bathroom counters regardless of whether the room had been occupied recently or not. At times she would give the counter a good cleaning, only to find that, in a matter of minutes the hairs would return, as if out of thin air.

On other occasions, the television would cut on by itself. Once, the housekeeper, deciding to do a preemptive move against the ghost, unplugged the television when she started her cleaning. Assuming this would prevent any messing around, she went to work and was shocked when it came on anyway! She checked to see if it was still unplugged and, despite the fact that it definitely was unplugged, the television remained on. She left the room for a moment to gather her thoughts and attempt to rationalize what had just happened. However, upon returning, she found the television had cut off by itself. One of the oddest things about this event was that static was the only thing to cover the screen, no matter what channel it was turned to.

On one particularly frightening occasion the housekeeper had pushed her cleaning cart into the room with her. While tidying up she had turned her back to her cart for just a moment, but was suddenly startled by a loud thud on the floor. She turned around to find her cleaning cart had been knocked on its side and was lying on the ground. Since she was the only person on that floor and it was impossible for such a heavily-centered object to have simply fallen on its own, the woman was uncomfortable enough that she left the room as soon as she could, figuring she was not wanted in there on that particular day.

It's possible that if the ghost in the room is in fact that of the murdered young woman she may roam other parts of the historic inn as well. Commonly reported by guests and staff is that a woman dressed in old fashioned clothing appeared in front of them, as if out of nowhere. She always seems to be a pleasant lady; of course, as soon as she is addressed she usually disappears.

Another member of the housekeeping staff had an odd encounter as well. She was walking down one of the halls and she noticed that a woman dressed in a rather out-of-date dress was coming down the hall toward her. The woman appeared lost and the housekeeper, in an attempt to be polite, offered her assistance. The woman casually turned toward her and said with a slight smile simply "no" and continued walking. As the oddly dressed woman passed, the housekeeper felt an intense cold sensation. When she turned around to look at the woman one more time, she was shocked and terrified to see the woman was not walking but floating down the hall — there was nothing below the ankles! After seeing this, it wasn't long before the housekeeper resigned her position at the Lake Lure Inn.

Shasta Seagle was a member of the housekeeping staff for over a year at the Inn and had heard her fair share of ghost stories from the older staff members. At first she passed them off as just that, simply long yarns people passed on to new employees to give them a jolt and welcome them to the team. However, before long, she started encountering the inn's ghost herself and found out some "long yarns" are true.

In such a large building members of the staff would often find themselves alone in sections of the Inn, which is what had happened to Shasta one evening; she was in the Spa. An uneasy feeling pricked at her as she went about her cleaning duties and despite the fact that she was alone, it almost felt like she was not. Shasta put her mind on her work, but that stopped when she heard a loud and "gravely" male voice say her name. This was all it took and she decided to call it a night (who can blame her!). Shasta later relayed this story to her supervisor, who merely laughed it off.

She didn't laugh for long; soon the supervisor encountered the same voice, except it was in the ladies bathroom. That day, Shasta's supervisor was feeling sick and had retreated to the bathroom to splash some water on her face when she heard a gravelly voice ask if she was okay. The first thing that went though her mind was that a man was in the ladies bathroom. She turned around to find out who it was, but found that she was the only person in the bathroom. In that moment, she became a believer of the existence of at least one of the inn's resident ghosts.

Other strange activities that have occurred on the property include a phantom man in the dining room that normally, but not always, seemed to appear by the fireplace late at night. Shasta heard the night auditor report seeing him standing in a black suit; he just stared off into the darkened dining room as if he was looking at someone in the darkness. The auditor commented that the man looked "as solid as anyone but gave off an 'unearthly feeling'." When the mysterious man is spotted, he is normally by the large fireplace in the dining room, but he has also been seen in random locations of the dining room: standing by tables or even walking across the room as if going to meet someone.

Most people who see him think the male phantom is the ghost of none other than Lucius Morse because of the similarity the apparition has to the painting of him that hangs in the main lobby. He has never tried to talk to those who witness him. Investigations by a paranormal team at the Inn last year produced some interesting EVPs from that area of the dining room; one was of a man telling the investigators to "leave!"

The auditor, along with others who are in the Inn burning the midnight oil, have seen another nocturnal specter. However, this guest is far less easy to identify. It descends the main staircase, but it does not walk. Rather it simply floats. Because it does not take the form of a person but simply a large smoky fog, it has been witnessed countless times on its trip down the stairs...only to dissipate when it reaches the bottom. Who this ghost was in life is not known neither is why it seems to be attached to those stairs. Possibly it is Dr. Morse simply choosing not to take a form while he does his nightly patrol.

The mist descends the staircase.

Some have reported seeing shadowy figures in random parts of the hotel, darting across the room or appearing out of the corner of an eye. Others have reported hearing the sound of a ball being bounced in the inn's basement, as if two children were bouncing it between themselves. Sometimes this is accompanied by the sound of children's laughter, but of course no children are ever found down there.

The first reports of ghost sightings at the inn came about twenty years ago, very soon after the inn was renovated and restored. Possibly the changes stirred up some lingering specters that before this had chosen to stay silent. Some also believe that some of the local haunts are not attached to the property, but possibly the antiques that are on display in the inn, which were added around the same time. The spirits could have simply followed them to their new home.

Regardless of where they came from the spirits seem to be a part of the hotel and are for the most part a very friendly bunch. If you ever find yourself at the Lake Lure Inn, keep an eye peeled for Dr. Morse, who seems to be still watching over his old place.

Old Wilkes Jail

Wilkesboro is located on the south bank of the Yadkin River and is the county seat of Wilkes County. It also hosts the yearly blue grass musical festival, Merle Fest. It is also home to its fair share of historic treasures that fill people with a sense of childlike wonder as they look upon them.

Old Wilkes Jail is one of those places that is an historic treasure. It was constructed in 1859, and due to the Civil War that started a few years afterwards, it housed Union prisoners during those first few years. However, it would be a prisoner from after the war had ended that would assure its place in North Carolina history and folklore for over a century.

Tom Dula (pronounced Dooley) was born in 1845 and, while growing up in Wilkesboro, fell in love with Ann Foster, a local girl; she loved him as well. Often they would spend nights together planning for their happy futures with each other. When the Civil War began in 1861, Tom followed his sense of duty by joining up with the Confederate Army's 42nd North Carolina infantry, leaving Ann behind for, what he assured her, would only be a brief time.

Ann was sure, as the first year without him turned into two and then three, that Tom would not survive the war, so she eventually gave up any hope of seeing her love again. She married James Melton, an older man and a local farmer. It is said she did not love him, but simply saw him as a stable future. Despite Ann's beliefs to the contrary, Tom did not die, even though both of his brothers did. Instead, he spent some time in a Union prison, but when the war ended, he was set free. He returned home to Wilkesboro, ready to find Ann, the love of his life, and start their life together.

It must have been quite a shock to them both when he arrived back home and finding out that she was married to another man. This did not keep them from being together; the two would continue to spend many nights together.

Ann, as it turned out, was not Tom's "one true love"; her cousin, 18-year-old Laura, was also someone he fancied and spent a few nights with. Eventually, he got her pregnant and made plans to leave with her in the night; he told folks that they were going to elope and raise their child together.

Tom and Laura would never be married; instead Laura would disappear while Tom stayed around. Originally the assumption was that she had simply run away without him. It was Ann's sister, Perline, who weeks after Laura had vanished, led a search party to a shallow grave that contained the young woman's corpse. Perline said that Tom had killed her and told Ann about the murder.

In addition to being shot, both of Laura's legs were broken. Also, she was found with the clothing she had packed the night she was supposed to run away with Tom. Finding out that he was the only suspect in the murder, Tom fled from the posse that was sent to arrest him. He did not make it far, only getting as far as Trade, Tennessee, before he was finally caught.

Tom was brought back and put on trial. His defense attorney was former North Carolina governor Zebulon Vance, who was so sure of Tom's innocence that he defended the case pro bono. However, no one else seemed to feel the same way about his innocence and Tom was found guilty, sentenced to death by hanging. On May 1, 1868, the sentence was carried out and Tom Dula drew his last breath.

As far as most of the people of Wilkesboro were concerned, a guilty man had gotten what he deserved, but justice may not be that black and white. Some believe Tom was innocent; there is a theory that Ann, in a fit of jealousy, carried out the murder that evening. Initially, she was implicated in the murder and spent some time in jail in the days following the discovery of Laura's body, but she was eventually cleared of all charges. During this time period, most people could not believe that a young woman was capable of such a horrible crime. There are some reports that on her deathbed Ann confessed to the murder of Laura, saying Tom was actually innocent of the crime he was convicted of. There is no way to verify that she actually said this; nevertheless, many believe she was definitely involved in Laura's death.

After Tom's death, he would soon become somewhat of a celebrity. It started with a poet named Thomas Land, who wrote a poem about the murder, which was later recorded into the song "Tom Dooley" in 1929 by Grayson and Witter. The song was rerecorded by the Kingston Trio in 1958 and it was the Trio's version of the song that would become the most famous. All this fame led to a movie being made in 1959, starring Michael Landon as Tom Dooley. All the poems, songs, and movies portray the common view that Tom was Laura's murderer.

Before long, Tom Dooley was not just a North Carolina story, but a national one as well. Most people maintain the thought that he was a cold-blooded murderer, yet others disagree with this view. Possibly even Tom himself, who now haunts the jail in which he spent his last nights on earth.

The Old Wilkes Jail stopped functioning as an actual jail in 1915 and was then apartments until 1968. As the condition of the building began to worsen, it was marked for demolition. Apparently the famous jail was on the verge of being wiped away from the face of the town of Wilkesboro when the Old Wilkes Company stepped in to save this historic landmark and prevented it from being reduced to a pile of rubble. They immediately began restoring the building to its former glory. Walls were repaired, period furniture was brought in, and historic pictures and paintings were hung on the walls.

In 1970, it opened up as the Old Wilkes Jail Museum and, as the staff and visitors would soon find out, Tom Dula was still around and apparently still angry about his death. Activity was reported within the first year of the museum's opening, as people were afflicted with a feeling of being watched, especially near the old cells (cold spots were very common around there).

Soon people would hear the sound of two men arguing from the upstairs cells. Possibly Tom has found another lingering soul (maybe a Union solider) who he has taken an extreme dislike to. Different folks hear different things being yelled back and forth, but it is clear the two are not happy with each other.

Tom also seems to be walking his death march over and over again. He is heard marching down the hall, dragging heavy chains behind him, no doubt heading to the gallows. Now Tom has never made an actual appearance in the jail, at least none that have ever been reported, but almost all those who believe the site to be haunted have no doubt that Tom still lingers in the jail.

It would not be hard to imagine way he has chosen to stick around the old jail throughout all this years. After all, it has been restored to the historical condition it would have been around the time of his death. In many cases of haunting, the use of authentic historical pieces can help trick the deceased into not realizing their time has come.

Chapter Two

The Piedmont

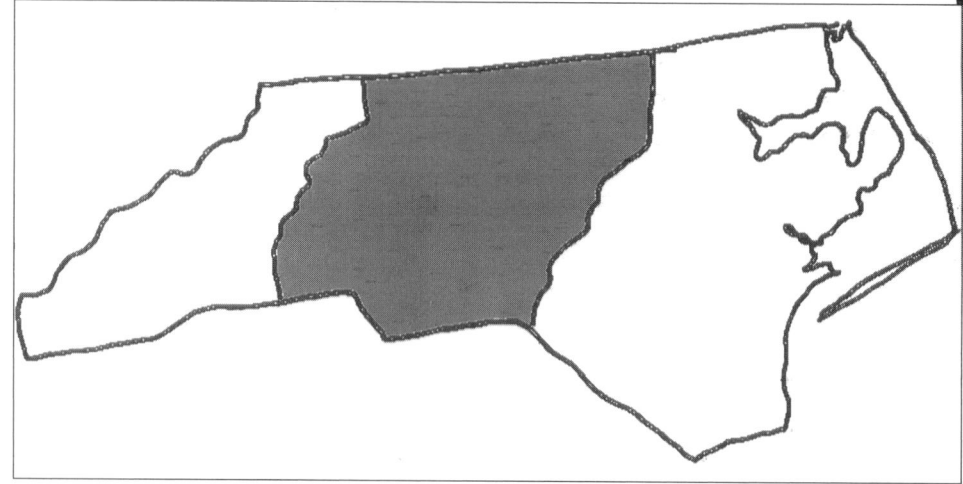

The Capitol Building

No longer the dominating figure it was when it was first constructed in 1840, the State Capitol building only stands ninety-eight feet from the ground to the top of its rotunda. The modern Raleigh skyline now dwarfs it, with the RBC building and the Clarion Hotel reaching much higher into the heavens than it does. Still the architecture of the historic building, along with its importance to state government, still makes it the centerpiece of Raleigh.

Anyone who sees the old girl can tell she is a product of another era of design — the building itself is cross-shaped with a large rotunda right on top. As I already mentioned, the construction was completed in 1840 at a cost of $53,268,234, which was over three times the yearly income of our state at the time. Obviously with that kind of financial investment it was a very important building for the citizens of North Carolina, then and now.

When the Capitol was first put to use, the branches of the State government operated out of this one building until 1888, at which time the state supreme court and the state library moved to their own locations. In 1965, the General Assembly moved into the aptly named State Legislative Building, so with all the roommates gone, the Governor's office is the only branch of North Carolina's government still housed in the Capitol building today.

Obviously, if I am mentioning the capitol in this particular book, you have by now most likely guessed that it haunted. You would be correct in guessing that, so good for you! There are many reports of the paranormal on the land around the building, so many in fact that once a year, on Halloween, a "ghost" tour is held in the building. The education staff of the capitol is helmed by Tiffianna Honsinger, who has not only collected all the reports of haunts, but has also done research on the legends and history that surround them. She was kind enough to share all her collected stories and research with me for this book.

The Capitol Building in Raleigh.

The most extensive accounts of the paranormal happenings come from (no surprise here) the folks who would spend most of their time there by themselves: the night watchmen. Owen Jackson was a night watchman for the capitol for fifteen years. Spending those evening hours alone, night after night, provided ample time and possibilities for Owen to have more than one encounter with the paranormal.

The one place Owen would most often hear an unexplained noise was the library. From time to time, he would hear something that sounded like a person slamming books on tables, though the room was empty. The first time Owen heard this, he was doing his regular rounds; he heard the sound of heavy books falling on the floor, so, assuming a shelf had collapsed or something else that could explain the sound of books crashing to the floor, he went to check it out. Owen entered the library and found everything as it should be. No book was out of place. No shelf had collapsed. It would not be the last time he heard this sound, but he soon learned to not get too worked up about it.

Whatever or whomever was causing the sound did no real harm. Owen was not the only one to hear the noises from the library; even during normal hours people would often hear books being slammed on the top of tables or on the floor without a single book actually having been moved. Various people also experienced other phantom noises and feelings within the library, including seeing apparitions that moved at non-human like speed across the room.

During his tenure as night watchman, Owen had seen and heard the gambit of paranormal activity occurring all around him. Not all members of the security profession have to deal with such disturbances, but Owen learned to take it in stride. The phantom noises range from a reoccurring scream of a woman that is heard often with no distinct point of origins, hearing the sound of someone walking up the stairs only to inspect them and find no one there, the distinct and unmistakable sound of window panes being shattered and the glass fragments hitting the ground only to find every window in the large building to be perfectly solid and not even a crack in them, and of course the sound of books being slammed down.

Owen managed to see at least one ghost instead of just hearing the silent interlopers. Owen's sighting took place when he saw the specter of a Confederate soldier through a window. It was a particularly cold evening and he was sitting in his car outside letting it warm up a little, but, as always ever diligent, he kept his eyes on the building the whole time to make sure no one was up to no good. He let his gaze look at the senate chamber window when he saw something that at first made no sense...and then made his blood run cold. There was a person staring at him through the window. Being a guard first and foremost, he assumed someone had broken in, but as he began to get a better look at the person standing in the window Owen started to notice something very odd about him — he was dressed in confederate military garb!

The man stood there long enough for Owen to get a real good look at him and to verify what he was seeing and then the phantom vanished into the pitch-blackness of the room. Owen needed no convincing that he had seen a ghost in the building, but, as duty dictated, he still had to make sure it was not a living person with an odd fashion sense. Owen checked all the doors to make sure they were locked; he verified no windows had been broken and then entered the building and checked its interior. Needless to say, he found nobody, let alone a Confederate soldier roaming the halls.

The ghostly confederate may very well be the cause of another paranormal phenomenon that took place within the senate chamber (this time with multiple witnesses). In 2004 and 2005, the Ghost Research Foundation performed investigations in the Capitol building. They caught some compelling photos and had a few interesting EMF spikes, but the most fascinating event took place in the senate chamber. To see if any of the lingering spooks were from certain periods they brought a laptop with a Civil War era music CD. Before starting the investigation they tested all the equipment, including the CD, and found that everything was in perfect working order. Naturally, everything should have worked fine.

They soon began their test; they started playing the music, all the music a Confederate would know and likely played just fine, but then the disc started playing the famous Union song "The Battle Hymn of the Republic." It did not even get two notes in before it jumped to the next track without anyone being near it. Like any experienced and levelheaded paranormal investigator, their first thought was the CD must have been scratched (even though only moments before the CD worked just fine). They tested it in the laptop again, but the CD was found to be perfectly fine, so they began the music again. Every single track played fine until they got to the Battle Hymn again. Just like the first time it jumped the track to the next piece of music. This continued to happen every time the investigators tried to play that one track. Later, after they were outside the building, they once again tried to play "The Battle Hymn of the Republic," but this time it played every single musical note without a skip or stall in the entire thing.

It is very likely that the same Confederate soldier Owen saw was not a fan of the Union military music and was most likely stopping it from being played in that room, which was no doubt sacred to him.

Now, you may ask, "Why would the soldier be in that particular place?" The most likely reason is that it is the same room that, in May 1861, the Order of Secession was signed, which removed the state of North Carolina from the Union and brought it into the Confederacy. It would seem at least one ethereal solider is still lingering in the room holding on to some old grudge, or at any rate really does not like "The Battle Hymn of the Republic."

Owen, the night watchman, is not the only person to experience the supernatural in the historic building. Raymond Beck, who worked for the county, has two notable experiences that have been recorded. Late one evening in 1976 Raymond was sure he was the only person in the building when he heard something he shouldn't have — the sound of someone's key jingling, which was then followed by the sound of a door opening and shutting. At first, Raymond was sure that another public servant or somebody like that was possibly coming in to finish up some work much like he had done. He went to check it out, only to find that the hallway was empty and there were no sounds of anyone walking away or being in the building at all.

Next, he went to check the door, which he was positive he had heard open, but found that it was locked just as tight as it had been the last time he checked it. Not sure what to make of this revelation, he began to head back to his work, but as he was doing so, he heard the exact same sounds again, but this time they came from another door. Raymond ran to see who was doing all this opening and closing of doors and key rattling, only to find that no one was near the door or even in the hallway. It would have been impossible for anyone to walk around in the empty building without being heard yet somehow this phantom set of keys and feet did just that.

In 1981, Raymond had another late night at the office that led to him experiencing another odd encounter. Around 10 p.m. Raymond heard faint music being played, but the thing that struck him as odd was how it seemed to be from a bygone era. He could not find the source of the music anywhere and when he attempted to locate its origin it would simply stop, only to start over again as soon as he went back to work. As the phantom music played and he went about his business, Raymond experienced an uneasy feeling that he was being watched. It would be hard to chalk this up to an overactive imagination; Raymond had spent many late nights working and had never before had this feeling that there were people around him he could not see. The music and the unseen peepers continued to bother him until, around midnight, he finally felt disturbed enough to leave.

Needless to say, an historic building like the Capitol building takes a good deal of care and upkeep. At some point in 1999, while some remodeling and maintaining was being done on the building, two carpenters saw something that left them scratching their heads. One day, as the fellows were going about their work, one of them noticed that the chandelier in the room they were in was swinging to the right and then back to the center. This was odd because there was no draft in the room, all the windows were shut, and no ventilation systems were on at that time.

There are a lot of legends about people dying or even committing suicide on the grounds of the capitol, but thanks to the research done by Tiffianna and the rest of the good people at the Capitol we know they are just legends. Tiffianna has researched the history of the Capitol down to the last details and informed me that there are no records of anyone dying on the premises of the building.

You may be wondering about now: So what does this mean for the ghosts of the Capitol? Who are these invisible office-mates and why are they hanging around there? Well haunting a location does not mean that an individual had to have died there. It just means that, in life, the location held a special importance for the person; whether it was the place they were happiest at or felt they did their most important work.

The paranormal investigation done in the Capitol in 2004 and 2005 concluded that the number of entities haunting the building was five, though there was possibly more that would come and go as they please. The only specter that has given any hint to his identity is the Confederate soldier in the senate chambers, who is possibly still standing guard to protect the room or to pay homage to a succession that he believed in enough for him to risk his life.

Mordecai House

Among Raleigh's historic landmarks and sites is the Mordecai House, which is one of its greatest. The Mordecai House is the oldest home still standing on its original foundation in Raleigh, but if that seems odd to point out, you should know the home of our 17th president Andrew Johnson was moved to the Mordecai Park from its original foundation, so not everything stays were it is built. Anyway, the oldest parts of the home were constructed by Joel Lane in 1785 for his son Henry Lane who he gave the house to as a gift.

The Lane and Mordecai family names are, in many ways, intertwined in Raleigh's history, as they are donating or selling lands to the ever-growing city whenever asked or needed. Henry Mordecai, the owner during the Civil War, donated land to be used as a Confederate cemetery. He also gave the land that was used as the city's first Hebrew cemetery.

As for why a home built by the Lane family is now called the Mordecai House, well, you would have to look at a gentleman named Moses Mordecai, a man who married into the Lane family not once but twice. Now that's determination! Moses first married Henry's daughter Margaret, but she eventually passed away, leaving Moses a widower. Still he wasn't going to resign to be alone for the rest of his life, so eventually Moses developed feelings for Ann, the sister of his late wife, and before long, they were married.

The modest Lane family home became the Mordecai family's house. Shortly before his death in 1824, Moses hired William Nichols, a well-respected state architect, to make the home even larger by adding four new rooms to the structure. The home changed drastically, not just in size but also in appearance. It soon had a Greek revival style, which made the home even more of an eye-catcher.

For a large part of its history, the home served as a plantation that consisted of around 5,000 acres and grew three main crops (cotton, wheat, and corn), which made the house a hub of daily activity. After his death, Moses's daughter Margaret took control of the home and after she died, it was passed down to her descendents; the last of which was Burke Little, who passed away in 1967. After this, the house went up for sell, along with its future and Raleigh's past, so the city of Raleigh stepped up and bought the home. They then handed it over to the Historic Sites Commission to ensure its preservation for decades to come.

The Mordecai Historic Park soon became a tourist attraction for those who were interested in the local history. As I have already written, along with the Mordecai House, the Andrew Johnson home was moved to the park as well to make it more accessible. Visitors could now tour two historical sites without the trouble of going to two locations. Both the homes and the beauty of the park draw countless people from not just North Carolina, but all across the country; it was visitors to the park that first reported odd happenings in and around the historic home.

It began like most paranormal activity with only slight signs that something in the building was not quite right: cold spots in hallways while the rest of the house was very warm; the sound of someone walking up from behind only to find no one around; brief shadowy figures moving almost too quick to see, but slow enough to be glimpsed. The people who witnessed these odd occurrences would tell the staff, which began seeing similar occurrences themselves. The ghosts were pretty uncommon at first, being felt or briefly seen only by a small handful of people here and there. As time went on, though, the entities seemed to get a bit brasher and began doing more to be noticed.

The ghost remained a mystery until at least one of them decided to show herself on quite a regular basis — a woman often seen on the stairs by the main entrance dressed in a gray nineteenth century dress. Most often she appeared to be walking down the steps. This specter does not just hang out at the stairs; rather, she also makes her rounds around the home and has been seen in hallways, the parlor, and through a window from the outside. One of the witnesses, who only saw the mysterious lady very briefly, figured out that the ghostly woman was none other than Mary Willis Mordecai Turk. Mary's portrait is on display in the home and looks too much like the apparition to be just a mere coincidence.

Mary is also thought be responsible for a more pleasant phenomenon: people taking tours of the house or even those who are locking up for the night report lovely piano music coming from the downstairs drawing room. No one is ever found playing and as soon as anyone goes to inspect it the music simply stops. Now and then Mary will start playing again as soon as her living guest leaves the room.

Mary also seems to be somewhat of a sensitive sort. Whenever someone in the house decides to make an unflattering comment about one of Mary's pictures, the picture in question always seems to be knocked off the wall and slammed to the ground. Someone cannot take criticism apparently, so keep that in mind when you visit the house.

There are reports of activity that does not seem to be instigated by Mary, which include the sound of a horse trampling on the grounds, though there are no members of the equine species on the premises. Folks who have been near the park at night have reported hearing the sounds of a horse-drawn carriage taking off from within its vicinity, possibly some spectral horse rushing one of the house's former residents to some destination.

This wonderful house is a piece of North Carolina heritage and is simply a must see for anyone who visits Raleigh. It is lovingly maintained and cared for by the proud people of the city it has been a part of for over two hundred years. While you are there, keep your eyes on the stairs, say nothing but nice things about Mary's pictures, and keep your ears open for some piano music. You never know when Mary may decide to let you know she is still around.

Queens College

Heading to college is something that many Americans undergo at different points in their lives; many colleges and universities have been around long before modern times. Queens College, in Charlotte, is one such higher education institute that has been around and helping minds cultivate knowledge over a hundred years. Normally students spend a few years taking the classes they need to graduate and then move on, yet at Queens College it seems some former student has yet to do this after nearly seventy years!

Queens College has not always been in the Myer Park neighborhood it is now located and it has not always been known as Queens College. It started its life as a college on 9th Street in 1857; its original name was The Charlotte Female Institute, not shockingly a school just for women. It would be moved to its current home and given the name it is known by now in the year 1912. The school was named Queens College in honor of an institution that had been built in 1771, which was called the Queens Museum, and also for Queen Charlotte of Mecklenburg.

The college would only have female students for a large majority of its existence, but in the years following World War II the first of many male students were allowed to enroll. Today, the school is bustling with young minds ready to absorb as much knowledge as possible. The coed student body traipses from class to class and socialize with their friends like college students tend to do, yet unlike most colleges around the state several locations around the school seem to have a touch of the ethereal to them.

Albright Dorm houses many of the school's students just as it has for decades. Normally after a few years or so these students will leave the dorm behind, but apparently, at least one student has stuck around for a few decades longer than expected. There have been a lot of encounters with this particular ghost, but little is known about who she was in life. It is believed she is the sad soul of a young student who had fallen in love with one of her female classmates, Julie, sometime in the early part of the twentieth century. This ghost, in life, did her best to hide her love from others, sure that they would not understand, especially considering the tensions of that era in American history.

She could not, however, keep it hidden forever and soon her parents, the people she feared the most discovering her desire, found out about her feelings. They, as she expected, did not approve of her feelings and let her know this in a heated exchange. The girl became distraught, torn between her feelings for Julie and her parents disapproval. She tried her best to figure out what to do, but in the end she did what sadly some do when things seem simply too painful — she took her own life by cutting her own wrist. She used her last ounce of energy to write Julie's name in blood on her wall and then died in her dorm room.

Losing a fellow student, especially in such a tragic way, is never easy, but life, like it must do, eventually returned to normal for the students and faculty, at least for a while. As new students began staying in Albright, odd occurrences soon started happening. Students would wake to the sound of a girl weeping in their room; assuming it was a fellow suitemate they would go to check on them, but never could find a physical source for the weeping. It would continue for sometime varying from a simple matter of minutes to even longer. Unlike many cases of ghostly crying, this distraught soul did not stop while people searched for her. She will cry as long as she chooses to and then fade into the ether, leaving behind some slightly startled students.

Sounds are not the extent of the ghost's manifestations, as she has appeared in more direct and upsetting ways to the students in the dorm. More than one student has reported entering their room to find the name Julie written in blood on their wall; it would have the appearance of having just been written only moments before. Normally this resulted in some panic since the students did not know who or why this was done, so they run to grab something to begin cleaning or to find someone to whom to report it. Yet, in both scenarios, upon their return, the wall is completely bare of any signs of anything being written at all.

Others have an even more direct sign of the distraught girl's wandering spirit — actually seeing her in their rooms! Students say that while studying or just relaxing sometimes they have their attention drawn toward a corner of the room by a sudden movement, expecting to see maybe a moth. Instead they see a young pale looking dark-haired girl walking into the bathroom or across the room. She is transparent and seems to pay those in the room no mind...and then vanishes with a flitter of the eye.

If the ghost haunting the dorm is in fact a distraught former student, I, for one, hope she finds her peace and has to wander the halls no more. For now, the poor girl still reportedly wanders the halls and makes an appearance here and there. Sometimes people will hear her, but she seems to be a relatively quiet specter as opposed to another one of the school's long-time guests.

The Wallace Dorm has a ghost of its own, but this one seems to be more about making a mess and noise than about anything else. There appears to be no origin for this ghost or any tragedies linked to the building, at least that anyone knows about. It just seems as if this particular poltergeist has picked this building for the heck of it. Students have heard the sounds of objects being broken in the dead of night only to find no tangible evidence of occupants or broken objects. The ghost seems to enjoy making destructive sounds without actually doing any breaking. Students who hear this often stress out about it because it is not some small clank or thud in the night, but a very loud sound of bulky or multiple objects being knocked off shelves or chairs smashing to pieces within close proximity to their beds.

Yet on other occasions it will rearrange the inside of student's dorms without making a sound. Sometimes a picture has simply been moved while at other times the room looks like a tornado has come though. People will hear loud footsteps walking down empty halls or knocks on their doors when they are already wide open. On other occasions they will hear the sound of a knock on the door that is actually closed. When they ask, "Who's there?", they will hear a friend's voice say, "It's me." Of course, not only is no one there, but also they find out that the person whose voice they heard had not been by their room at any point.

While this noisy ghost mimics voices and trashes rooms, it has never apparently shown its face to anyone. It seems to keep to the invisible realm instead, leaving whatever he or she may look like to the imagination. Although this specter is a nuisance, it has never shown any mean or hostile intentions toward the students. More like a phantom prankster, it seems to enjoy getting a jump out of them.

Another sadder spirit in the halls of Queens College is that of another student who reportedly committed suicide, though the reasons are unknown, within the halls of the school. He never speaks or makes any noise; no one would know he was there if they didn't look right at him. He appears as the lifeless body of a young man who hangs from the banister of a stairwell. He appears so much like a real person that on several occasions the police have actually been called because people believe a suicide has just taken place. However, the spirit never lingers and disappears within a matter of moments, thus he's long gone when the authorities arrive. He has been seen on multiple occasions over the last few decades, but, again, his identity and the reasons behind why he is seen hanging is not known.

The resident spirits of Queen College are somewhat a noisy and often alarming lot; still they never seem to pose harm to any who encounter them...unless you count losing a little sleep now and then.

McAlpine Park

Located in Charlotte is a city park used by locals for everything from jogging, dog walking, or a casual stroll yet many do not feel particularly comfortable in a certain section of the park. Situated in this park is a very old, abandoned mill house. For decades those who walked by it always felt a sadness emanating from it, though most assumed it was a sentimental reaction to the sight of the old building. It would not be until the early part of the 1980s that a terrible discovery would be made at the site: underneath the mill two human skeletons were found!

This revelation caused a great deal of local interest. After being moved and examined by a medical examiner, it was determined that the bodies had been buried under the mill for at least fifty years. It was also learned that both were in their early twenties when they had died, one was a male and the other female. The female happened to have a silver heart necklace still around her neck. The decomposition had made determining who they were and how they died impossible at that time, but it is reasonable to believe they were likely a couple, possibly two lovebirds taking a stroll though the park. Most likely they met someone with ill intent, so they were shuffled loose of this mortal coil and hastily buried where no one would look for them.

Two dead lovers.

Soon after the bodies had been given a proper burial, those who took advantage of the path that went by the old mill started seeing something quite odd as they went on their morning runs: they saw the perplexing sight of the deceased couple walking hand-in-hand. They both have been described as having dark hair and are completely solid, though their clothing often seems dated (most pinpoint it to around the 1930). Yet it's only when the couple disappear right in front of the witness's eyes that they realize they have just seen the park's resident ghosts. They seem to simply be enjoying each other's company and a nice stroll along the path, with eyes normally set on only each other.

Those who have gotten a good look from the front of the two specters say that the girl is wearing a silver heart necklace around her neck. Apparently it must have meant a lot to her in life, as she still carries it with her in death.

The Cajun Queen

When people see The Cajun Queen for the first time, they may think that they are looking at someone's home, but it is not — at least not anymore. The Queen began its life in 1918 as a private residence, which would explain its outside appearance; it would continue serving as one until the 1960s, when it was purchased by a local man who turned it into a place of business, which has continued ever since in different forms. For the last twenty-five years the building has served as The Cajun Queen. It should be no shock than that it is a Cajun themed restaurant, located in the historic Elizabeth neighborhood of Charlotte, a well-known and beloved eatery where people gather to enjoy the unique atmosphere and the wonderful meals offered. However, it also may have other features that most restaurants don't have: a few ethereal restaurant patrons.

The spirits that seem to be lingering around the old house appear to have no area that they will not visit and often pop in just to let their presence be known. An old-fashioned southern woman has been seen sitting at the bar in an outfit from around the nineteenth century. She is normally seen making herself quite at home, but will disappear whenever someone tries to approach her. She is also believed to be responsible for the odd incidents that occur around the bar, such as glasses being moved or just vanishing altogether. People say they feel someone touching their hand, only to find no one near them, or hear a woman talking to them only to find that no one was.

Robin Eiden has worked at The Cajun Queen for the better part of the last decade and has personally had more than just a couple encounters with the house's unseen residents. She told me about the problem that used to occur with the upstairs women's bathroom. It was a common complaint that it was always frigid in there, no matter what time of year, regardless of the temperature outside. Along with cold temperature, there was an uneasy feeling that trickled through the room, like you were never alone even when you were.

In recent years the coldness and uneasiness has seemingly stopped, and the room has returned to an average lady's room. Quite possibly, that particular phantom has decided to haunt somewhere else at the Queen. The staff of the Queen often changes in an upstairs storage closet, and like the ladies bathroom there is a general feeling of uneasiness when the staff is in the room. Robin says that it became so uncomfortable that for a time no one would change in there by themselves; rather, they made sure they were in a small group before they went in.

The electronics in the building also exhibit its share of problems. Frequently, the lights would flicker on and off at random times. Yet, there have been no electrical problems ever found with the lights or wiring to explain why this occurs. The Cajun Queen has owned several ice machines in the time Robin has been employed there and they all seem to develop the exact same problem. The ice machines seem to spit ice out at random times; at first this seemed to be a mechanical problem and not a paranormal one, so when the machine would not work properly no matter what was done, a new one was purchased. Assuming that the problem was now solved the odd behavior of the former machine was forgotten, but, of course, when the new one started the exact same behavior it stopped seeming like a simple mechanical problem. As for why the machine is a target, no one seems to know.

Other phenomena around the restaurant include an upstairs window fogging up even when the weather is warm and sunny. If wiped clear, the window will just fog back up. Many staff members have witnessed this phenomenon. The basement of the Queen is often reported to radiate with an aura that induces an uneasy sensation when people are left down there by themselves and odd noises and whispered voices seem to come from the darkest corners of the room.

All the activity in the former home is largely believed to be the work of one entity that used to be a former resident of the house — that of a southern belle who is often seen by the bar. It seems the bar was constructed in what used to be the master bedroom of the house and some think she is not happy about this. She looks like a simple woman who is (as I said earlier) dressed in a rather dated outfit. Some say she is just up to some fun, but some believe she is truly unhappy with a bar being in her house. One theory is that, in life, this woman was a teetotaler and in death still wishes to give those who enjoy a good drink a hard time about it.

Whoever is haunting The Cajun Queen, the staff and customers do not seem to be bothered, at least not enough to close down, and find her to be a part of the décor of the historic home.

Gimghoul Castle

It is really hard to live in Chapel Hill and not hear about the famous castle or the secret society that owns and uses it. Located atop Piney Prospect Hill behind UNC's Chapel Hill, Gimghoul Castle is home to the Gimghoul Society, which is made up of UNC Chapel Hill students and alum. Founded in 1889, it started out as the Dromgoole Society, but they soon changed their name to add a more creepy feeling to the group. The famous castle, which is also known as the Hippol Castle, was constructed in 1924.

The location was not picked at random by the secretive group either — they formed around the legend of a former student who met a tragic end. His name was Peter Dromgoole (hence their original name) and the castle was built on the location where he was killed.

Peter Dromgoole meets his fate.

There is legend in the area behind the University of North Carolina in Chapel Hill; long before a castle was built there, a tragic event was reported to have taken place in those woods. In 1833, Peter Dromgoole, from Virginia, fell in love with a local young lady, known as Ms. Fanny, but the only problem was that he was not the only man interested in her.

The other suitor, whose name has been lost to time, finally challenged Peter to a duel of pistols; they met on a spot of land known as Piney Prospect.

The duel took place, but it did not have a happy outcome for Peter — he was mortally wounded and fell on a nearby rock splattering it with his blood. The legends say he was not dead, but actually dying. His own friends, probably afraid of the repercussions of aiding a duel, did not help him; rather, they dug a shallow grave and buried him while he was still struggling to live. The legend goes on to say that Ms. Fanny never found out about Peter's fate (although some versions say she in fact was at the duel) so she would come and wait for him at Piney Prospect as she wept.

Now a lot of what is known has been passed down via word of mouth and no doubt there have been some creative tweaking here and there over the years. Some things are known as fact though: Peter Dromgoole did exist and was in the Chapel Hill area during the 1830s. He is known to have disappeared in 1833, never to be heard from in this region, although some claim that he simply fled to Europe.

It would be about ninety years after the duel took place that a secret society of students and alumni from the university would build the famous Grimghoul castle in the area that Peter was supposedly shot and buried. The castle itself, which is built in a pre-Norman English style, adds to the heavy air around the locally famous spot.

The rock that legends say Peter hit his head on still sits there and is still stained by his blood from the day he died. People who have ventured to the location have reported seeing a young man lying on the ground loudly moaning in pain, but as soon as anyone draws near he will simply dissipate into mist. Others have claimed to only hear the moaning of poor Peter, though they have never actually seen him. Still, there are others who have reported seeing a young woman sitting on the ground sobbing very loudly. This is thought to be, without a doubt, Ms. Fanny, who still waits for the man she loved, having no idea that she haunts the same grounds as her former love.

The castle and the grounds are private property owned by the Grimghoul Society, which has a very strict no trespassing policy, so no one has really been able to see if Peter's ghost still lingers today. Nevertheless, his legend will live on, at least as long as the Gimghoul Society is around.

The Carolina Inn

Chapel Hill serves as home to one of this state's most prestigious colleges, the University of North Carolina at Chapel Hill; it is the university that owns the Carolina Inn, which is, in its own right, a prestigious institute with its own interesting history.

The construction of the hotel was started in 1922 by an alumnus of the school, John Sprunt Hill; Mr. Hill was very fond of his old school and wanted to be sure it provided comfort to fellow University alumni who might pay a visit to the school. The Inn would first open its doors in 1924. It combined the architecture of elegance with that of southern comfort to create a hotel that stood apart from any of the others in the area. The Carolina Inn would officially be given to the university in 1935 in the form of a donation from Mr. Hill, who only asked that the profits from the hotel go to support the school's library, which held a special place in his heart.

More than likely, most people have, at least once in their lives, stayed in a hotel that is just so nice and comfortable that they simply never want to leave. Dr. William P. Jacocks had that feeling for the Inn, but he more than just wished he could live there — he actually did it. He spent his last twenty years of life in Room 252 in the Carolina Inn, no doubt working up a good size room service bill. Dr. Jacocks had worked most of his life for the international Health Division of the Rockefeller Foundation, but when he finally retired in 1948 he checked into the Inn. He was very well known around the hotel by staff members and returning guests and seen as a wonderfully friendly man with one heck of a sense of humor. He was known to pull quite a few practical jokes on the staff during his time as a resident there. He was much cared for by everyone who met him and was considered another perk of the hotel.

All good things must come to an end and Dr. Jacocks was no exception to this rule. In 1965, he passed away and a sad air fell on the Carolina Inn, as everyone was positive they had seen the last of Dr. Jacocks and his practical jokes, but this may not have been the case after all.

The ghostly activity began being reported in Room 252 almost immediately after it was rented out again, but this was not a "I want to scare you haunting." Instead, it seems that Dr. Jacocks's sense of humor had followed him to the next world.

Guests who stay in the room often go to sleep with an object such as a wedding ring or watch on the table next to them on the night stand and by the next day it will have disappeared. Of course panic (especially for wedding rings) is the first response, but this ghost is no thief; he simply moves the objects across the room to places like under chairs or on top of the television. Those in the room have no idea how, why, or by whom the object has been relocated, but it does not take long for them to learn about the resident spook and his harmless playful sense of humor.

Now and then people will awake and prepare to take a refreshing morning shower...only to find the towels, bath mats, and shower curtains completely rearranged from the night before. Towels that where once folded may be scattered across the floor, the bath mats will be folded on the counter, and shower curtains will be wrapped around the rod very tightly. Why he does all this activity is not known for certain, but, again, it is most likely simply for the fun of giving the current resident a nice jolt.

Guests have also have been locked out of Room 252. Back in the days of regular keys, many a guest had a nearly impossible time getting the door to unlock when they would attempt to turn in for the night. On one particular occasion, the door could not be opened; it was so stubborn that, after all other solutions had been exhausted, the staff finally had it taken off the hinges. When examined afterwards, no one could find a reason as to why it would not unlock. The Carolina Inn has converted to the use of electronic keys, but it still endures the occasional guest having one heck of a time getting into their room.

There are other things that Dr. Jacocks is believed to be responsible for that is located outside his old room. He is thought to be responsible for the male voice heard all across the third floor of the hotel. People will hear a deep-voiced man coming near them, yet either no one is around or those who are swear it was not them. It is never quite clear what he is saying; some say they hear him call them by their names while others say it sounds like he is trying to hold a conversation with them. He also is heard walking around the halls of the third floor or in his old room of 252, seemingly just casually enjoying a stroll as he no doubt did while he was alive.

There is no disputing that Dr. Jacocks was a beloved long-time resident of the hotel while he was alive and many believe he continues to be so in death. A friendly specter who seemingly does nothing more than play a joke on occupants of his home for so long, having never been anything but a host with a slight sense of humor to his guest. He is still reported to mess with people in and around his room, so if you ever find yourself in Room 252 at the Carolina Inn, remember not to lose your temper at his practical jokes; they are all in good fun.

Latta Plantation

What a breathtaking vision the Latta Plantation Park is! Far more than just an historic building, it is an entire center just perfect for sightseeing or even those who wish to sign up for horse-riding lessons. These are just a few things Latta has to offer. It is located in Huntersville and serves a very vital purpose as a piece of living history in these modern times, giving those who so desire a chance to see southern life in a different era.

Latta Plantation is not new to the block, so to speak, and to place it in perspective, it was around before Abraham Lincoln was born. In 1799, James Latta bought one hundred acres of land from Moses Hayes; along with the land he got a modest home that Hayes had built on the property. Latta had no desire to settle on anything that was just "modest," so he began building his family an elegant plantation. He also started adding more acres to his land. Between 1800 and 1817 he purchased an additional 600 more acres from the surrounding area.

As his plantation grew, so did his family, money, and the slaves he owned to work the fields. In the early days of 1800, the Latta family had only two slaves, but at the height of their plantation they owned over thirty. Their most well-known slave was a young woman who was purchased when she was only 14; her name was Sulky. In the very same year the War of 1812 (that would be the year 1812) started, James Latta purchased Sulky from a sheriff in South Carolina. She would be a constant sight in the Latta home for many years to come and, for a while, actually having a room in the house until she moved into the kitchen, which in those times was separate from the main house.

In 1837, at 82 years old, James Latta passed away. His wife, Jane, would continue to live within the Latta Plantation for two years after this, and then in 1839 she moved closer to her daughter and son-in-law, leaving the plantation behind. After Jane's death, the home went through a slew of different owners for the next century that included her son-in-law and even later Duke Power. It was 1973 when the plantation was added to the National Registry of Historic Places and only two years later it would become a Mecklenburg County living history museum, but the years had been not as kind as they could be and the old girl would need some help.

In 1976, the historic site underwent what would be the first of two restorations to the home (the second in 2004). The aged home was brought back to its original glory, ensuring that even more generations would be able to experience the feel of walking though a piece of North Carolina history.

Today Latta Plantation is a well-known historic site that hosts many events and reenactments. It has also become known for paranormal phenomena that have been witnessed by staff members and visitors alike. On any given day of the year the Latta Plantation is buzzing with all kinds of people going back and forth, possibly touring the house or giving the tours. It should be no surprise then that the number of encounters with the ghostly inhabitants of the home are numerous.

Kristin Toler, executive director of the historic Latta Plantation, has heard all the stories that have been told over the years and when asked if she thought the plantation was haunted she wasted no time in answering me with a definite "yes." She and the rest of the staff at the historic site were very generous and shared with me a collection of ghostly encounters they have compiled for their own ghostly tours; thanks to their efforts, I share those stories with you.

The best stories to start with should be from outside the building and are reported by people who spent the night outside on the grounds of the plantation. Before the restoration in the 1970s, Boy Scout troops would often camp-out all around the home, the house dark and empty during those evening hours. The only people around were the intrepid young scouts and the scoutmasters. The only noises anyone expected to hear were of nature's symphony, crickets, and other creatures of the night, but instead they often heard unexplainable sounds coming from the empty home, the most common of which was shattering glass. This was not a solitary glass-breaking sound, but repetitive and loud enough that the scouts checked all the windows from the outside to see if any had been broken and found them all very much still unbroken. This was baffling for them; there was definitely the sound of glass shattering yet the only earthly place that it could come from had all its glass accounted for.

This Boy Scouts troop's odd encounter was over thirty years ago, but there is a more recent outdoor encounter from another group of campers at a 2007 outing. A group of Civil War re-enactors were spending their evening like the real Civil War soldiers would have — sleeping in their tents, embracing the elements — but it was not just the natural world around them that night. Many of the campers reported seeing shadowy figures move around the camp during the evening.

Now, once you get inside the house, the number of ghostly encounters goes off the charts, in a manner of speaking.

Wayne Thomas was a former employee of the Plantation; among the duties he performed was the shutting and locking the doors after all the tours had ended for the day. He nearly had a constant problem with the front door; he would lock it and begin moving towards other regions of the house when, often, he would hear a loud "clunk" from the front entrance. Curious, Wayne would go back only to find the front entrance unexplainably unlocked. No one else was near the door and the speed in which it was done made it highly unlikely that anyone could have left without Wayne noticing.

In the mid-1990s, site director Elizabeth Myers was performing a Christmas candlelight tour of the house. Everyone was having a wonderful time experiencing what it would have been like to have a Christmas in the 1800s, so you can imagine their fright when a mysterious thud came from the attic door upstairs. Elizabeth laughed it off, so the rest of her group did as well. Their laughter only lasted a few moments because another sound arose, much harder to shrug off. It was the sound of small feet running on the garret floor followed by the unmistakable sounds of children's laughter. No one knew exactly what was going on, but here is what is known: there were no children on the tour (keep in mind children are not fans of no electricity) and the garret was pitch black so there was no way anyone could be safely running around up there. Everyone on that tour heard the kid's laughter. It was not a matter of what they heard, but simply how.

One of James Latta's children died while they lived in the house; Ezekiel Latta was the youngest child and the only son, but spent most of his life battling consumption, a childhood ailment that left him very weak. He was sent to Bethel Academy in South Carolina when he was nine, but within the following year Ezekiel died; his body was sent back to his family in North Carolina for burial. Could it be that the young boy's spirit never found rest and that he has returned to his childhood home and chooses to have the fun he was unable to in life?

Someone messing with locks on the doors would have to get pretty aggravating and phantom children running around in a darkened house could be pretty scary, but in 2000 staff member Amy Bruining had two notable encounters in the home. Amy was sweeping the parlor, making sure the home was as clean as possible. She knew for a fact that she was alone in the home and at the time she was fine with that; after all, some people believe that solitude is nice at times, so she was shocked when she heard someone with heavy feet walking on the second floor. Amy knew the layout of the home like the back of her hand and knew that the *person* was walking from the master bedroom to the children's room. The phantom walker repeated the path a few times before simply stopping. Maybe this was the ghost of James Latta, checking on his children in their room.

Amy would have another interesting moment with one of the house's resident ghosts. This time she had a whole third grade class as fellow witnesses. It was about one year later when Amy had the honor of showing some young school children, on a field trip to the Latta Plantation, around. She was telling them some interesting facts about the home when there was a loud crash on the second floor. Amy did not pause for a second; she knew her first responsibility was the children so she continued with the tour. Amy figured she knew who was responsible anyway; her first suspects were not ethereal but feline. During the previous summer, the staff adopted two cats, who were adorable but also troublesome if they ever got in the house; this is what Amy figured had happened.

In her mind the only thing that could have crashed like that was the Chinese water beaker in the master bedroom. Undoubtedly, one of the cats had jumped on the table and knocked it over. She waited until the tour took her up to the second floor before trying to get the cats back outside. Walking into the master bedroom, she expected to see a shattered water beaker on the floor and possibly a cat with an innocent look on its face, but the beaker was still safely on its table and the cats were nowhere to be seen. She began to search the upstairs as she continued the tour, but, bewilderingly, did not find anything broken. By then, she was even more baffled and, almost as if mocking her for suspecting them, she looked out the window and saw both of the house cats playing outside in the yard.

In December 2004 another staff member, Kristin Toler, was in the main entrance of the house setting up for Latta Plantation's Candle Light Christmas program. It was the middle of the day and Kristin was putting up some decorations around the front windows. She had been so wrapped up in her current task that she was not sure if she was in the house by herself or not, so when she heard noises from the second floor, she figured it was a fellow staff member.

Someone was walking around upstairs, which did not seem odd, when she heard dresser drawers open and close. She thought to herself, due to the heaviness of the footsteps, that it must be the farm manager, Ken Holmes. Deciding to try and take advantage of his presence, she yelled up at him to ask about his lunch plans. She hoped to talk him into ordering hers, along with his, to save her the trouble of going out and getting something. Kristin waited for a reply, but none ever came; she knew he should have heard her yelling. She knew that if he had walked away she would have heard him.

Kristin decided to stop her work and see what he was up to, so she walked up the second floor, expecting to see him right away. She searched the whole top floor and did not find anyone at all! No Ken. No fellow employees... No one at all! Once the thought of this possibly being paranormal in nature entered her mind, she decided to vamoose and leave the entrance only partially decorated, figuring she would come back when a living person was able to keep her company in the house.

Kristin and Amy are not the only staff in the house to encounter a phantom walker in the halls at the Latta Plantation. Volunteer Betty Pierce has heard it on more than one occasion. Betty is positive the person roaming around the house is James Latta. She had noticed that it normally appears when work of some sort is being done to his old house as if he is making sure no one does anything he does not approve of. She has heard him on several occasions; one particular incident she recalled happened near the rear door, which she had just checked to make sure was locked for the evening. While in the adjoining room, she heard the door open and close followed by heavy footsteps walking in. She knew that the door was locked and no one should be able to get in without a key; she turned around and was looking directly at the back door that was still closed. She made one more check to verify the door was locked and it was, so Betty went back to her duties. You get used to it when you work at Latta Plantation.

Karen Lane is another volunteer at Latta and a vital part of what makes the place run smoothly, often leading tours through the house. In 2006, on Mother's Day, she was doing just that. She had finished a set of tours and was talking to some folks from the last group on the front porch when a loud thud was heard from inside the house. Signaling Dwayne Thomas, who was outside the house with them, she told him about the sound. Dwayne unlocked the door and they went in to find the cause of the noise — they tracked it down to the house's parlor.

The mirror that should have been over the tea table was now in the middle of the floor. Finding a mirror fallen over is not that odd; I have destroyed many a mirror. However, in this case it was not simply a mirror falling forward. Not only was the mirror completely intact, but it was also lying an impossible distance away from where it had been in the first place. It was in the center of the room face down, so it could not have fallen like that. Someone or something would have had to drop it at that spot. In addition, the tea table that had been in front of the mirror still had all the items sitting on it — it would be kind of hard for a large mirror not to take a few things with it when it falls.

James Latta may still be hanging around his old bedroom, or it may be someone who really likes his old stuff. Sitting against the wall in the master bedroom is one of James Latta's old walking sticks. The odd thing is that it seems to refuse to stay where it is placed. Witnessed by multiple people, it has on what seems to be its own accord started to wobble and fall forward away from the wall. One staff member had an even more unsettling experience involving the cane, which he found laying on the bed. Assuming it had been left there by a fellow staff member, he picked it up, placed it back against the wall, and walked out of the room while tending to other duties. Moments later he returned to the master bedroom to do one more check. He was shocked to find the cane was laying back on the bed! No else was up stairs with him and he knew he did not imagine moving it the first time. It seems someone preferred the cane on the bed, not against the wall.

The dancing cane is not the only reported activity in the master bedroom. Tour guides often experience weird feelings when they are near the bed. While giving tours, the staff usually ends up next to the bed. It is while standing there people feel a tightness of breath or a strong nausea. It sometimes feels so strong that some guides have nearly had to stop their tours, but generally the feeling fades quickly after they leave that particular area.

The stairs seems to be a favorite location of one of the ghosts: an apparition of a woman dressed in nineteenth century attire has been seen numerous times descending the stairs. Who she was in life could easily be Jane Latta or possibly one of her daughters; none of them passed away in the home, but it is possible one or more of them have chosen to return to it after death. It was on these stairs that a paranormal non-believer received physical contact from one. Joyce Jamieson, another member of the Latta staff, was walking in the rear of a tour group one evening. They were heading down the stairs, as she felt someone lean against her from behind; she figured that it was a group member needing to regain their balance. Joyce turned around, expecting to see a living person, but was instead met with only the sight of the empty stairs. She was at the very end of the group so there was no one who could have been leaning on her.

Another specter on the stairs (maybe James Latta again) is a gentleman with mutton style sideburns that is often seen ascending the staircase at a fast pace. He has even been known to address visitors in the house, but not in a welcoming way. He will order them to "leave this house." If this is Mr. Latta, he may not be aware of his home's open-door policy to the public and is unhappy with people trampling around the property.

Sulky, the Latta family's best-known slave, seems to still linger in her old room too. Sulky lived in the house for much of her life with the Lattas; although, later she married and had children of her own. It's in her old room that Kristin Toler received a sign from Sulky; she had walked through the entire second story of the house and made sure all the furniture was in place, the tables were straight, and the beds were still made. She went through Sulky's room and straightened up her bed. Later that day as she went back though the room, the first thing that caught her eye was the condition of Sulky's bed. It had been unmade! No one beside herself had been in that part of the house and no one would have any reason or desire to do such a thing.

Another recurring phantom of the historic site is a woman dressed in yellow. She is normally seen entering the house through the front door or right inside the front of the home. She normally seems to have the demeanor of someone coming back in after doing some kind of yard work, which seems to be indicated by the fact that she is sometimes seen with a basket full of fresh cut flowers.

There seems to be no doubt in any of the employees' minds that Latta Plantation is home to more than just one restless soul. Why they have chosen to stay is anyone's guess. They seem to be all over the house and the grounds, making noises in empty rooms, appearing on stairs, and moving objects around in the bedrooms.

The Latta Plantation and surrounding park are definitely worth the trip! The history and natural beauty along with the possibility of a ghost encounter make it a great destination.

Piney Grove Church

They are known by many names. Often they are called "Houses of God" or "Sacred Ground," but they are most commonly known simply as churches, a place of sanctuary from the evils of the world. No one ever really gives much thought to the possibility that they could fall victim to a haunting. However, the abandoned Piney Grove Church seems to have done just that.

Piney Grove church was built around 1884 as a predominately African American church and there is a graveyard located about fifteen feet away from the building. The church served its flock lovingly during its entire run, no doubt serving as a place of refuge from the racial tensions of the day. The cemetery has graves as old as 1901 and as recent as 1998. The two most frequent families you will find buried on the grounds are the Reids and the Propsts, as these were two of the main families that attended the church.

The church was abandoned shortly before the new millennium. Most likely, the reason had something to do with the ever-growing housing developments that were sprouting up near the church. It was left so abruptly that the church was still set up for Sunday services: a large Bible was open and hymnals ready for a service that never came. The years have not been kind to the old church; vandals have smashed and destroyed much of the interior of the building.

There have been reports of paranormal activity in the cemetery for nearly a decade. The most commonly seen specters are black shadowy figures that are seen darting from grave to grave. They have no distinguishable features and never remain in one spot for more than a second. They seem to stick around only long enough to scare off would-be trespassers. Anyone who ventures into the cemetery almost always report being overwhelmed by a very uneasy feeling, as if they are being told they are not welcome there.

The ominous feelings and shadowy figures are also sometimes accompanied by disembodied voices. Visitors to the site often hear what they describe as whispering that seems to be coming from everywhere and nowhere at the same time. It normally seems inaudible, but is generally loud enough to rule out any trick of the mind. Other times people actually hear very clear and loud talking; this usually involves very angry warnings toward trespassers that include "Go away!" and "You don't belong here!" The fact that the spirits notice and communicate with visitors would indicate an intelligent haunting at the site.

A large amount of the information I have gotten about the haunting at Piney Grove has come from veteran paranormal investigator, Kimberly M. Kenyon. Kim is a member of the New London paranormal research group called Southern Spooks. Her team has done several investigations at Piney Grove and they believe that it is haunted.

Piney Grove Church.

Kim and her team have done EVP work on their trips, often picking up human and what some may call inhuman haunting sounds. They have detected many voices from the graveyard, sometimes repeating what others have said they have heard there, usually along the lines of "you don't belong here." The most troubling piece they collected is from the old driveway in front of the church. They recorded something that sounded like an inhuman growl. It sounded almost like a dog growling, but no dogs were anywhere in the vicinity, at least no living ones. Some researchers believe these kinds of noises caught on tape can be the sound of what is called an "inhuman haunting" or "demonic," which is a spirit that was never a living human and normally seems to have negative intentions towards the living.

Southern Spooks is not the only group to have picked up something odd in that location. Many people have felt intense cold even in the summer months in front of the church. Like with the graveyard in back, there is a general feeling of apprehension as if you are being watched. This may be caused by the possibility that some people have used the abandoned building as a site of occult rituals or other forms of séance, which can often lead to unwanted guests.

As for the church, a few people have ventured into the building and have come back with at least a few encounters, some of which I will relate. First let me make it very clear that the church is not a well-preserved historic location with a staff, like many of the other locations in this book. Piney Grove Church has been left to the mercy of the elements and vandals, so, for your own safety, I would strongly advise against entering the building for any purpose. Those who have entered have all obeyed the first rule of paranormal investigation (and elementary school field trips), which is of course the buddy system!

The reason it is always important to not go to any location by yourself is for simple safety precautions. If you where to be hurt, it is a definite plus to have a friend along to help you. In a place like Piney Grove, which has been militantly destroyed and ramshackled (no this is not the work of angry spirits but everyday humans with apparently too much time on their hands), there is more than one way to be hurt and an extra set of hands can be invaluable. The church is reportedly home to at least four spirits, but not all of them are "friendly" ones. Among the tools investigators have used at the site is EVP, with the most troubling sound picked up on the recorders many would describe as "demonic" — an inhuman growling in multiple locations in and around the building. Along with what is picked up by scientific equipment, many sensitives have picked up at least one very angry entity in the church; this entity is apparently extremely unhappy about people entering the church.

So who could these restless souls have been in life? Who is it that has become an almost ethereal watchman of the old church? The most common belief is that these spirits are former members of the church's flock and who are now interred in the cemeteries. It could be they are perhaps unhappy with its current condition. It does stand to reason that if they held the church dear in life, then seeing it not only closed but also defiled by people with no respect for the generations that met there and paid their respects to the almighty would upset them. Maybe they do their best to ward off anyone they think may be possible vandals.

Still the spirits could be around for other reasons. Maybe they even haunted it while it still functioned as a place of worship. The former congregation never mentioned any haunting, but it is well-known that the church was abandoned in a hurry. Possibly the invisible members of the church was part of the reason for the move.

The haunting at Piney Grove is still reported to be ongoing as the people who venture to it still see the figures in the cemetery and odd sounds and noises come from inside the building itself. It is a sobering fact that even houses of god (or in this case former house of god) can still be homes to lost souls, with no way of knowing anything about them. The only thing we can do is pray that they finally find their peace.

The Devil's Tramping Ground

You cannot talk about the supernatural in North Carolina and not discuss the infamous Devil's Tramping Ground, a staple of North Carolina ghosts and folklore for hundreds of years. It is just a forty-foot barren circle in the woods south of Siler City. Still, it has been a source of speculation and ghost stories since the first settlers came to Chatham County, long before the days of the American Revolution.

In the modern world this patch of dead earth is called the Devil's Tramping Ground; the common folklore is that this is where the Devil comes to plot evil deeds against the world of man and all his works. He would walk in a circle as he contemplated dastardly schemes, his infernal steps killing all the plant life in the circle path. Now I find it slightly presumptuous to assume that the devil comes to the Tar Heel State to do his wicked thinking. Is that really someone we want hanging around North Carolina on a regular basis?

Now this is not the first legend to explain the barren patch of land; in fact, the devil was a latecomer to the theories to explain the dead earth. One of the earliest ones included the battling of two Native American tribes; the losing tribe was so badly beaten that they fled to the outer banks where some say they became the Croatian Indians. The spot of the battle was so drenched with the blood of pointlessly wasted life that the gods decreed nothing should ever grow in the spot again as a consistent reminder of the cost of war.

As society and science grew across the state, more people wanted to find a natural explanation for the Tramping Ground so scientists of all kinds answered the call. A United States Geological survey could find no definitive reason why the circle is lifeless, although it has been discovered that there is an abnormally high level of salt in the earth in that spot. Many believe that the high salt content — and not some supernatural fiend — is behind this local legend. Nonetheless, the fact that it takes the shape of a nearly perfect circle is very perplexing.

Now, having a barren patch of land is not enough to label any place as haunted, so what else happens to give the Tramping Ground its paranormal reputation? One of the oldest claims of the Tramping Ground is that any object left in the circle overnight will be moved outside its perimeter by the next morning. This particular phenomenon has been reported since the earliest settlers to the area noticed stones placed in the circle would be moved aside the next day. Until a few years ago people reported items being moved from the circle by unseen forces during the night. In recent history constant gatherings at the site have caused large amounts of litter to be left in the Devil's Tramping Ground, so it seems to remain where it is laid nowadays.

As increasing numbers of people became curious about the Devil's Tramping Ground, they started spending the night at the dead patch of land. One of the older claims is that those who dared to spend the night were always insane by the next morning. It was believed that the people who stayed overnight would see the Devil himself and see his true face; this would make their mind break and leave them crazy for the rest of their earthly days. These days people spend the night at the Tramping Ground all the time...usually to test the stories and they all seem still sane the following morning. Now, people who choose to spend the evening there never claim to see the Devil, but many of them are sure that they have had paranormal encounters while they are there.

One particular story involves a young lady named Sarah, who, along with some of her friends, decided to spend the night. They set up a tent and got ready to enjoy a fun and "spooky" evening. They, like most of the people who did this, had no real belief in the possibility of a ghost or ghoul haunting the site; it was simply a local spot of folklore that made it corny in a cool way. After setting up the campsite, they began to relax and have a good time.

After getting comfortable, they heard the sound of some people talking from outside of their tent. As she described it, "It was like inaudible whispering." Of course, at first they assumed that someone else was out there; after all, it was a hangout for many people who were drawn by the legends. When she looked outside the tent, she found the whispering had stopped and there was not a single soul around.

It was only after returning to her tent that she had another pretty scary shock: the sound of people walking by her and even hitting her tent from the outside, which picked up in ferocity after a few minutes. Sarah and her friends waited for it to stop and as soon as it did they ran out to see who it was. Once again, they found the area completely devoid of life. Shortly after this, she decided she did not care to spend the remainder of the evening there and packed up, figuring she now had seen what the Tramping Ground had to offer.

Sarah and her friends are not the only visitors to the site to report having their campsite being physically attacked by invisible fiends. Other Devil's Tramping Ground visitors also claim to see shadow men, spirits made of complete darkness who move extremely fast, darting in between the surrounding trees and running by tents. They seem to enjoy attacking the tents and creating scary sounds that come from the surrounding darkness.

It is hard to say if the Tramping Ground has been haunted since the first legend arose about it; however, in the last few years the site of the Devil's Tramping Ground has become one of occult rituals. People who are lured by the appeal of the legends will come and perform séances or other similar ceremonies in the patch of dead earth, assuming the place has some special powers. This could have brought the supernatural to the site if it was not already there in the first place.

The Devil's Tramping Ground has been a part of North Carolina before America was an independent nation, and is the home of many legends and folklore. You may wonder whether or not it really is haunted. I believe it is. Not because of the dead land that has always been there, but because of the people who have tried to contact the spirits there.

Some must have succeeded! Having been brought there, they have chosen to linger for their own reasons. If you ever choose to visit the Devil's Tramping Ground make sure to enjoy yourself and allow yourself to be immersed in the folklore that has made it so famous. Regardless of whether you see anything paranormal or not, it is truly worth the visit.

Victor Small House

Located in Clinton, North Carolina, is the former home of Victor Small. It is currently the home of the Sampson County Art Council. The people who presently work there have, for some time now, had the feeling they are not alone in the building; footsteps in empty rooms, disembodied voices, and objects that seem to take on a mind of their own are some of the peculiar activities that go on, but the ghost is not feared and there is little doubt about who this specter is. It's none other than Victor Small!

Victor R. Small was a doctor who spent the nearly fifty years of his days living in Clinton, but originally he lived in Kentucky. Victor was not only a doctor, but also a veteran of "the Great War," which of course we call World War II these days. He was also a published author of mostly works of poetry, but his best-known piece is his memoirs that revolve around his days at Gallipolis State Mental Hospital. The title by today's standard would most likely seem offensive coming from a doctor, as it was called: *I KNEW 3000 LUNATICS!*

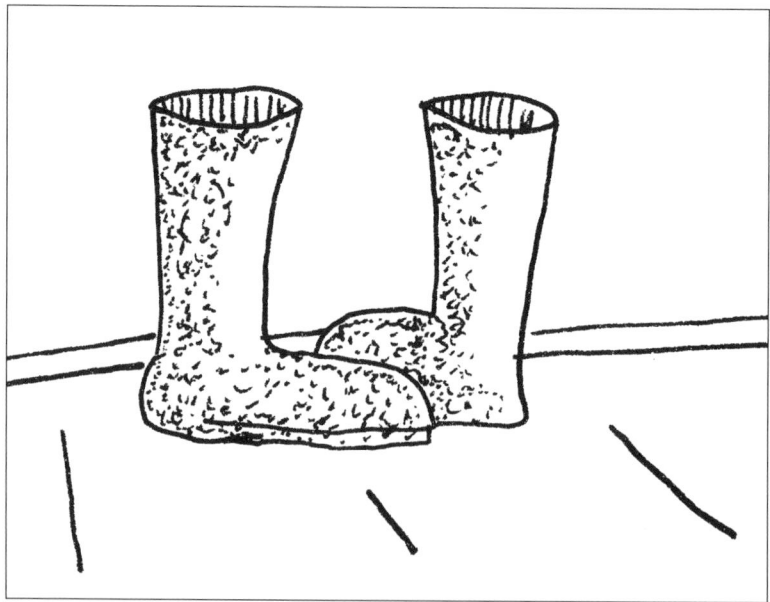

It was while he fought in Europe during the war that Victor met his wife, Susan C. Jacobs, who, at the time, was a Red Cross nurse. Immediately, they seemed to fall in love with each other and quickly entered a relationship. In 1920, they became husband and wife and moved to North Carolina. They lived in Raleigh at first, but, in 1923, Victor moved them to Clinton, where it did not take him long to find a place to become the family home.

What is now known as the Victor R. Small House was actually built nearly fifty years before he ever even saw it, constructed by its first owner, Abraham Hobbs. The house went through a few owners before Mr. Small purchased it in 1923. It was a widower, Mrs. Bettie S. Matthew, whose husband Leamon Matthew had lived in the home with her until he passed away, who did not want to stay there any longer. She sold the house and the lands to the Small family. Within the first year in the house, Victor had restoration work done to bring it back to its full glory. He ended up spending a small fortune to transform the home into his vision, making it truly his.

The people of Clinton soon came to know two things about Victor. One was he had great compassion for the poor and under privileged often helping them beyond the call of duty, usually without any form of payment, because he believed that helping people was more important than money. The other was his fanatical love of art, picking only the best pieces to hang in his home and painstakingly deciding the best placement for them. Before too long, he was lovingly called "Doc" around town, as if he was a family friend instead of just another doctor.

Yet, some say that he was not loved by everyone in his life. It is believed that Victor and Susan did not have a storybook marriage, often fighting over every little matter they could, which included where pictures should be hung in the home. Victor would hang a painting in one location and Susan would move it to a spot of her choosing while he was away.

With all his talents, compassion, and even marital problems, Victor remained one of Clinton's most beloved citizens. In 1971, as he drew his last breath in the back bedroom of his house, he would give the town one last gift: his home. As I have already stated, Victor was an art fan, but he feared that others were not and that future generations may miss out. Already noticing the declining interest the youth had in it, he gave his home over to the city of Clinton, asking that it be used for art. He also asked that only his bathroom remained unchanged because it is where he did his best thinking while he soaked in a good bath.

As I have said, it has become the home of the Sampson County Art Council, doing what the former owner wanted, which is making sure people maintain an interest in the arts. Still, since the very early days of

Victor's passing, people have gotten the distinct feeling he has not chosen to leave yet. Like many older homes, the house is prone to perfectly natural sounds caused by age; wood settling or a draft causing curtains to move a little, but Victor's old home has more than that.

The house has its share of unexplainable noises. The sounds of doors closing when none have been moved or someone walking down hallways that are empty are some of the activities. One of Victor's personal belongings that was left in the house is his pair of boots; they sit on display as you enter the building. One day, as the staff unlocked the door and began entering the house, they immediately noticed the boots. One had completely turned around during the night, in what should have been an empty house. All the employees were positive that when everyone left the evening before everything, including the boots, was in its correct positions. Why someone would rotate a boot around is hard to say. It could be that Victor (or possibly his wife) is still unhappy with the home's décor. It also may be the cause of the other moving objects in the house, including the portraits around the home.

The painting and pictures are not just slung on a wall any which way (like those in my apartment), but are carefully arranged by staff members just like Victor did while he was alive. Apparently, though, someone in the house does not care for the placement of the paintings. On a number of occasions employees have found paintings that have been switched in positions. Of course, the first assumption is another staff member has moved the paintings and they make sure to ask everyone, but no one has ever taken credit for the rearrangements. Is it possible that Mrs. Small still wants the home to be decorated as she would have wanted and refuses to let a simple thing like death get in her way?

Chapter Three

The Coastal Plains

Stonewall Manor

Stonewall Manor is synonymous with Rocky Mount. When I was growing up there, I heard many stories about the Manor from many local residents. Everyone used to joke about it having a few ghosts, but I was never sure how serious they were because everyone likes to tell a ghost story or two once in a while.

The home, a massive former plantation, sits off the U.S. 64 bypass. The house, itself, is in the middle of a magnificent oak grove, encompassed by a very large granite wall. It goes without saying that this stone wall is how the manor got its name. I know, what a shocker.

Bennet Bunn, a local businessman, first built the house in the 1830s. He had it constructed by the banks of the Tar River. Bunn had inherited the land from his father Benjamin Bunn, who passed way in 1814. Bennet wanted to use his new land to construct a large plantation to ensure his family's financial security. At the height of his affluence, he owned hundreds of acres and around one hundred slaves, causing him to have one of the most successful plantations in the entire state at the time.

Stonewall Manor

In 1849, Bunn passed away and his property went through multiple owners until the abolition of slavery towards the end of the Civil War. In 1916, Rocky Mount Mills purchased the property and the first renovation was performed on the aging antebellum house. In 1975, only one year shy of the United States bicentennial, the home came into the possession of its current owners, Nash County Historical Society, which has done everything to protect and maintain Bennet Bunn's old home and make sure it does not get lost to time.

I first saw Stonewall when I was a child living in Rocky Mount, as my parents were driving past it. It sat there, so massive behind its wall and oak trees. I remember thinking I could not imagine someone living in a house that large. As a child, I was amazed by the sheer size of the house, but also a little scared because it had a reputation for being haunted. The house didn't look creepy or anything, but it was off alone by itself and the antebellum structure of the house seemed terrifyingly alien to me. I was just a kid after all.

My mom told me the ghost stories of the house went back to when she was a young girl in high school. People would dare each other to go to the house at night believing they would see a ghost. She never did nor did she put much thought in the stories, saying that it simply came from the size and relative isolation of the house.

I did not do any research into the home when I lived in Rocky Mount and for the most part never really gave it a lot of thought. It was shortly after starting on this book that I wished to explore the stories and history of the home, wondering how real those old ghost stories were. I began by researching any historic accounts of haunting at the Manor. Initially, I was unsuccessful, but then I contacted some of the manor's staff.

Lauren Filliettaz, the Nash County Historical Site Coordinator, has never experienced anything herself, but has heard of other encounters with the resident spirits, which she was kind enough to relate to me. She told me that many of the long-time volunteers each had a story or two to tell about a ghost in the house.

Among the ghosts on the grounds, there may be phantoms of the Confederate army. Lauren informed me of a piece of local history from during the Civil War: near the end of the war, the Union army, on its way through Nash County, burned down the Rocky Mount Mills. As they left, they marched over Stonewall Manor's grounds. At another time Confederate forces also marched a very similar path over the estate. This may help explain two of the encounters Lauren relayed to me.

The countless acres that Bennet Bunn owned have long since been developed for the modern world. One section now contains houses that are filled with happy families that possibly enjoy having such an impressive neighbor as Stonewall. Like most neighborhoods in America, you have those who love to get out and embrace the natural world. One of the women who lived in the neighborhood was out walking her dog when she experienced something shocking. It was a route she had walked on many an occasion so she must have felt like she knew every twist and turn, but she was certainly in for a shock this time. As she walked by Stonewall, she looked over and saw a Confederate soldier on the grounds, but he was not alone — he had what the woman could only assume was some sort of Native American guide with him. She did not know what to make of what she was seeing; possibly she thought at first it was re-enactors or someone who just really got into history. She knew it was way too early for anything to be going on at the manor and once they vanished before her eyes those thoughts were discarded.

She told the staff at Stonewall about what she had seen, not sure what to make of it. No one had any explanation as to what she had seen except to tell her she must have seen a ghost.

The dog walker was not the only local resident to witness Civil War ghosts on the former plantation. A man who lives right behind the massive house was throwing a party in his backyard. He was performing the time-honored tradition of snapping pictures of those having a good time, hoping to get them in an embarrassing pose. During the party nothing seemed odd; it was not until he got his pictures back a few days later that he received quite a shock — one picture had part of Stonewall's yard, but it also showed something he knew could not be there at the time: Civil War soldiers marching across the yard! He knew that no activity of any kind was going on at Stonewall at the time and was positive he would have remembered seeing Confederate soldiers marching next door. He later received verification from Stonewall employees that no events of any kind had been preformed that day.

It seems that the outskirts of Stonewall are still littered with the soldiers of a war that ended almost a century and a half ago. It is possibly that these ghostly soldiers are the result of a residual haunting, marching the same land over and over again.

Lauren also told me of an odd phenomenon within the house on the third floor, which seems to be the center of the house's activity. During the Christmas season a few years back some of the decorations in the house left pine straw all over the third floor. Employees were quick to sweep it up, but the straw was not that easily removed. The pile of pine straw returned to the same spot on the floor the next time someone entered the room. It was disposed of again, yet it returned time after time in a pile on the floor. This caused a bit of frustration and uneasiness to those who had to keep removing it, but eventually it stopped reappearing to everyone's relief (especially those who had to clean it up).

The most famous specter in the house is that of a little boy whom numerous witnesses have seen. Thanks to the late Mr. T. E. Ricks, who was a dedicated staff member of the Manor, the boy's name is now known to be Ronald E. Stevens. He died when he was five years old from spinal meningitis in 1938. This little boy has been seen by more than a few witnesses, but none more credible than three separate Rocky Mount police officers. Stonewall is equipped with a modern security system that includes motion detectors in case of break-ins or vandalism. It is not unheard of for the motion detectors to go off even when the house is completely empty (of the living at least). Obviously, when it goes off, a member of the police force will head over to make sure no one is up to any trouble. On three separate occasions the officers who arrived on the scene saw someone in the house: a small boy standing in the window. It turned out, after further inspection, that there was no one in the house. It goes without saying the little boy did not stick around to answer the police officers' questions.

Re-enactors also saw this same little boy during an historical function on the premises in 2006. They reported seeing a small and somewhat sickly looking boy in the house while they prepared on the third floor. He looked at them with a curious and somewhat sad look on his face and was dressed in dark clothes that seemed a tad unusual for such a young boy. They assumed he was there with someone, but he vanished from the room though no one saw him leave. After asking about the child, they learned that he was not there with anyone and not a single soul had seen him since he vanished.

T. E. Ricks was an admitted skeptic about ghosts and other paranormal phenomenon. However, he compiled a few of the stories he heard over the years and the following are some of those accounts.

He once had a young woman who was a definite believer in the paranormal inform him that she had seen the ghost in the house on more than one occasion. Humoring her, he asked the woman to share it with him. She told him she had taken up the hobby of driving her car up to the house at night and spend the whole evening looking at the house to see if any ghost showed up and, according to her, they certainly did. The first encounter she described was of an apparition she saw through one of the windows in the third floor: "she" walked back and forth in front of the window holding a baby she seemed to be trying to rock to sleep. This particular spirit is an unknown. Who she was in life is a mystery. She seems to not be as vocal or up-front about being in the house as some of her other roommates and she is not commonly seen or heard in Stonewall.

The other household spirit she witnessed during those evenings was also a woman, but this one was a little more vocal. Like so much of the house's activity this ghost chose the third floor as her stage. She walked out onto the third floor balcony, but she did not just stand there — she let out a high-pitched scream and slowly her apparition, along with her scream, simply disappeared back into the darkness of the night. Possibly this was the same specter who held the baby the previous night, screaming over a tragedy that had befallen her in life or maybe she was trying to let the young woman witnessing it know she did not like being watched.

Mr. Rick's first personal experience took place on the third floor of the antebellum house. In the mid-1990s he had a persistent problem with the back door on the third floor: every evening he would personally lock the door and then take the only key to the door, walk it down to the basement, and place it in a safe place, which is exactly where he would find it the following morning. Yet he was baffled when he would find the door unlocked day after day (for well over a year).

The only person in the house who came in before him was a Dr. Margaret Battle who, along with her maid, would often handle the small cleaning tasks every morning around the house. Mr. Ricks asked her if she or anyone else had been getting the key and unlocking the door for any reason. She informed him that she was not and no one else had either. What made that even more frustrating was whomever was doing it would had of have been doing from the inside because it would take a thirty-foot ladder to do it from the outside. The door kept up with its refusal to be locked; he even came in to find the doorknob dismantled and scattered across the floor. Finally, whichever of the spirits was messing with the door, decided the gag was getting old and finally stopped. There is no doubt that Mr. Ricks enjoyed this pleasant change of events.

This was no doubt an odd experience for him, but his second personal encounter is even more fascinating. He wrote it down in his own words after it happened. This is his personal account of what transpired.

The other instance in which I have some personal involvement occurred recently at our annual Christmas open house. The event was cosponsored by the Sons of Confederate Veterans and they had a re-enactment going on during the weekend. There were a number of re-enactors on hand. One of the 'soldiers' and I had visited together on the main floor and he had gone alone on up to the third floor. After a few minutes, he called to me from the head of the stairs and said, "I suppose you know as much about Stonewall as anyone around, don't you?"

I answered, "I suppose so."

Then he asked, "In your research of the house, did you ever read or hear of a deal involving a small child there?"

"Well, yes I have, why?"

"I think I know what room the child died in," he said.

"Which one?" I asked and he responded, "The back room on the west side."

"Why do you think it was that room?" I asked.

As we had been carrying on this conversation, he had been coming down the stairs and by this time he was standing in front of me and he said, "When I stepped to the door of that room I felt a very strong presence of a child in distress."

Then I said that I didn't know if the child died in the house or what the circumstances of its death had been; though as I remembered the story it was a fairly short but devastating illness and I hastened to add that it was not early in the history of the house.

He responded with "oh no, it was after the turn of the century."

I asked him which sex was the child and he answered immediately "a boy." I asked if he had a feeling for its age and he quickly replied "5 or 6 years old." And then he said the little boy was lying curled up on the floor by the window looking out and when he approached, the child turned his head, looked at him in a piteous manner as if he had hoped he would come but was not at all sure that he would and whispered, "You came, you came."

The man was obviously moved by the experience and seemed hesitant to talk about it, almost as if by doing so he was betraying an intimacy that he had shared with the long-dead child. I questioned him further and asked if he had a feeling for what time of year this had occurred. He said he did not. Then I told him that I knew the little boy had a sister still living in the area and it would be interesting to know if she knew what room he died in or if he died at Stonewall. Then I realized that I had momentarily forgotten the family name of the boy. I could only remember the sister's married name, not her maiden name. I disclosed my lapse of memory to him and asked if he had a feeling for the family name. Without the slightest hesitation he answered, "Their last name started with an 'S.'"

As we talked, we had moved towards the ground floor and I remember we were descending the stairs when he offered this information. I immediately proceeded to where Dr. Margaret Battle was sitting, knowing that she was familiar with the story — in fact, it had been from her that I had learned of the death of the child. As I approached her, I asked if she remembered the name of the family who had lost their young son while living at Stonewall.

She answered, "Yes, it was the Stevens family." If I had ever had any doubt as to the sincerity of this individual, it dissolved at that moment. This man was from out of town; he had no way of knowing anything about the death of this child. In fact, I doubt if there are even a half dozen people still living in Rocky Mount who know of that death.

I called the sister that night. She was 12 when the death occurred. It was her room in which the "soldier" had seen the apparition and she said her brother was four years old. She thought he died in the hospital, but wasn't sure. She mentioned a friend who would probably remember. I called her the next day and she confirmed that he died in the hospital as best she remembered, but she had no documentation to prove it.

I asked if she remembered what time of year it was and exactly what year. She did not know. I asked the sister the same question and she had thought it was late fall. The reason I had asked this question of the "soldier" — and the sister and her friend — was because the porch just beyond the room was used as a sleeping porch during the hot summer months, and if it had happened in the summer then the child could conceivably have been on the porch on the other side of the window of that room. I also asked the sister if her little brother spent a lot of time in her room. She first said "no," but then she added that the stables would have been visible from the window and "Son" loved to watch the animals being worked.

The episode continued to fascinate me and I suddenly thought, "Wouldn't it be weird if this had happened on the anniversary of the death of the child, but no one could tell me when that was. Frankly by now I was quite touched by the whole thing and was becoming obsessed with getting to the bottom of it, so I drove to Pineview Cemetery and rode all over the old sections without finding a stone marked 'Stevens.' I had all but given up when I spotted it in the distance after starting to crisscross my original path of travel. I approached the plot with some feeling of anticipation, parked, and got out of my car. I knelt and read the stones: that of the father and the mother and then that of Ronald E. Stevens, Jr. who was born on August 17, 1933, and had died on November 23, 1938, at age five years old — the age the "soldier" had cited — not the age the sister had remembered. It was not the anniversary of his death, but interestingly enough exactly two weeks after the fifty-eighth anniversary of it.

Lee Stevens Gravely told me her father never got over the death of his son. Shortly before he died in 1967, she asked him something about her little brother and her father simply said, "I can't talk about it."

Ronald, Jr., called affectionately "Son," died tragically of spinal meningitis while he, his parents, and his sisters Ann, who was just a year older than he, and Lee, who was some seven years older, were residing in Stonewall. Ronald Stevens, Sr. was associated with Rocky Mount Mills, having joined the company in 1933, the year his son was born. He later became Assistant Treasurer of the Mills and jointly ran the daily operation with Hyman L. Battle. Lee told me she had fond memories of Ann and "Son" crawling up and down those winding stairs, their little bottoms twitching back and forth clad only in their diapers.

The family friend, Nancy Newby, remembered "little Ronnie" as being a darling, sweet, lovable child who tended to let his slightly older sister, Ann, dominate him. She remembers an occasion when the Stevens family was visiting her and they were sitting on the porch. Ann, for some reason, slapped Ronnie and the father told his son to slap her back, but be wouldn't and he climbed into his Daddy's lap and told him, "Daddy, I can't hit her."

I really don't know what conclusion to draw from this whole experience other than to say that I truly believe that some people have an ability to communicate with the past — I don't have that ability, but I respect and to some extent admire, those that do."

As I have already mentioned, Mr. Ricks has passed away and is deeply missed by his former co-workers and friends at Stonewall. His accounts of what happened are made more interesting by the fact that he was a declared disbeliever in ghosts, but even he thought this phenomenon was a little more than odd to just be something forgotten and swept under the rug.

Stonewall is open to the public on select days of the week and serves as host to countless functions in the Rocky Mount area including weddings, reenactments, and art shows. It has recently been added to the Historic Albemarle Tour (HAT), which is a selection of North Carolina historic sites spread out across seventeen counties. As one of the most real preserved antebellum structures left in the state, it most certainly belongs in this tour.

MacHaven

MacHaven House appears out of place in Rocky Mount, North Carolina, on 306 South Glance Street. It is a large brick mansion cut off from the surrounding homes by an impressive red-brick wall. Built in Georgian style during 1905, it completely dwarfs the homes that surround it in the growing area even though it once sat on the outskirts of the community. Over the centuries the town grew around the massive home, but it does not blend into the neighborhood.

MacHaven

A local businessman, James Hines, built the mansion for his wife Mary Matilda MacEntire (say that three times fast). Mr. Hines's money came from his business of selling ice (yes I said ice because before the days of refrigeration ice was still needed for a lot of things, but was a more expensive item to get a hold of). Mr. Hines's business venture had an even more long-lasting impact on the town. If a person ever found their self in Rocky Mount, spending a long duration of time waiting for a train to pass by, they could thank Mr. Hines's ice and coal business. It was his business that played a major factor in causing them to build the tracks in the first place.

After Mr. and Mrs. Hines died, the home was given to their daughter, Maryanne, who married into the Robinson family. The house would be home for generations of Robinsons until 1991 when it was sold to a local business man named, H. I.

The Robinson family never experienced any paranormal activity in the house, at least none they ever told anyone about. Mrs. Erwin Wilde was the granddaughter of James Hines and the last member of his family to own the family home; by 1991, she was an elderly woman and also good friends with a local businessman by the name of H. I. Tharrington; H. I. had been looking for a location to start a restaurant and catering company and Mrs. Wilde was ready to sell her family home to someone she trusted to take care of it for her.

It was only a matter of time before the final papers were being signed; the last details were actually being overseen in the house. It took place during a bright and beautiful day and the inside of house was as quiet as a grave. An ambiance of solitude and peace seemed to encompass the entire building. It was while he was already mentally figuring out the layout of the restaurant that H. I.'s peace was shattered suddenly by a loud buzzing sound that came from all over the mansion. The noise lasted for only a short time and finding what the sound was coming from was no hard task, but the real question was how?

The cause of the ruckus was coming from the old servant buzzers that were in almost every room of the house (normally near anywhere the lady of the house would park her butt). The only problem: all the buzzers had been disconnected for over a decade! An electrical problem seemed nearly impossible. This particular event never happened before or after, but only during the one time the house was being sold from the family that had built it, lived in it, and cared for it for eighty-five years. Was it possible that some unseen residents did not like the house leaving the possession of the Robinson family? Others say it was a sign of approval since they waited until the papers were signed to welcome the newest owner of the home, but...only the spirits know for sure.

The protest or approval from the ethereal realm was not a deterrent for H. I., as he began the process of transforming it into a place of business. The main house's first and second floors were converted into elegant dining areas and one modest small wait staff kitchen. The old carriage house, which was about twenty feet from the main building, was turned into the primary kitchen where the majority of the cooking and prepping would be done. It is very commonly believed that any change in a place's appearance can stir up the spirits that have stuck around after death; they see the world that the cling to changing around them and it makes them want to speak up.

My oldest sister, Lisa Ward, worked as a waitress in MacHaven for a number of years. Nearly from the start, she would often be in the building by herself to do the prep work for the evening's dinner crowd. It was during the winter of 1993 and Lisa was alone in the house and the doors were all locked. While upstairs setting coffee cups and saucer on the table, she heard the unmistakable sound of children laughing coming from the first floor of MacHaven. Her first thought was maybe the nearby Braswell Elementary School had let out and some children had somehow gotten into the house, but it was way too early for school to be out and all the doors were locked tight.

She inspected the large staircase, which is where she thought the sound had come from, but neither the top nor the base had any sign of anyone having been there. She checked the entire house, but it was empty and all the doors were still firmly locked with no sign of anyone having entered the building from any entrance.

Lisa is not the only one who has heard these laughs; the laughter of the phantom children would come and go during any time of day or night, sometimes accompanied by the sounds of running and playing through the building. This would not be the extent of the ghostly activity.

More than one employee would have all their hard work messed up by invisible pranksters. The dining room would be set up: all the place settings ready and all the napkins folded. The waiter or waitress would leave the area for just a minute and sometimes have a surprise waiting for them when they got back. Sometimes it was the silverware off the table, the napkins unfolded, or even all the chairs pulled out from under the tables. It seemed that someone liked making the wait staff job a little harder, but it did seem like the work of some prankster kids.

The lights around the house would sometimes like to cut back on after being turned off. Things of frustration for members of the staff as they would walk by rooms that were moments before pitch black now bathed in light.

Mark Brown, a former manager at MacHaven, worked there tirelessly for many years after the restaurant opened. He spent whole days on the premises doing anything that needed to be done. He had heard the people talk about the ghost of MacHaven, but never put much stock into such nonsense. One night, Mark was helping lock the place up after a busy day. He was about to make sure all the upstairs dining room tables were in order when he heard loud noises coming from the small kitchen in the main building. His first thought was some lingering member of the staff was making a mess and decided to head down and make sure they were going to pick up after themselves.

He walked down the side stairs, which came out right by the small wait staff kitchen. When he entered the kitchen, Mark noticed that the kitchen was dark and empty, so he cut on some lights to look around but didn't find a single thing out of place. There was nothing on the floor, no broken dishes; it was as pristine as it had been earlier that evening. Mark never found a reason for what he heard that night; he was left with only the supernatural possibility.

The main house was not the only place where there was activity; the kitchen staff in the former carriage house also had their share of encounters from unseen visitors. The unimpressive white flat room building sits adjacent to the brick wall around MacHaven and is a complete contrast to the majesty of MacHaven itself.

Often, the kitchen staff would come in several hours before the restaurant would open for the day and stay long after it closed in the evening, normally assuming they were alone. Chefs, cooks, and dishwashers all reported ethereal late night visitors in the kitchen: the sound of someone walking on the gravel outside the kitchen, the door being opened, and the distinct sound of someone walking in on the hard concrete floor was very commonplace. The kitchen was too small for anyone to hide in and the gravel that covered the whole parking lot made it impossible to leave without making a lot of noise, yet no one ever saw this person who kept entering the building.

When they left for the night, one former cook happened to look up at MacHaven and see a faint light coming from the window. The rest of the house was dark yet something that resembled a candle-like light was glowing in the highest point of the house. He knew the entire wait staff and management were gone for the evening. He stared at the pale light, thinking maybe some outside light source was just reflecting off the glass, but he could absolutely tell that it was coming from the interior of the building, not the outside. It suddenly disappeared, leaving the window pitch black again...possibly the specter noticed he or she was being watched and did not care for it.

MacHaven eventually closed its doors because of the lack of business to afford the large cost of upkeep and not due to any paranormal shenanigans. The home was added to the national historic registry in 1976, so the building is not going anywhere. It sits waiting for the next owner to come along and try their hand at caring for it.

The Prince Charles Hotel

Fayetteville is North Carolina's fourth largest metropolitan area; it is only a brief distance to Fort Bragg and Pope Air Force Base, which gives it a large amount of military traffic. It does not have the ocean or the mountains, but it's still a grand city with many historic sites, including the Civil War Averasboro Battlefield and the 82nd Airborne Museum. The city is named in honor of French general Marquis de Lafayette, who was of great importance during the Revolution.

The Prince Charles Hotel.

One of Fayetteville's oldest treasures is the elegant Prince Charles Hotel, a hotel constructed in the colonial revival style. It was the early 1920s and all over the country there was a feeling of wealth and decadence, and Fayetteville was no exception to this movement. The construction of an eight-story hotel was started. From the start the Prince Charles seemed built to last; she survived the dark days of the Great Depression, the stressful times of the Second World War, and even a fire that ravaged many other buildings in the area. She continues to stand as a proud part of her city.

The Prince Charles, with so much history to it, has seen its share of dark times; these moments have left their mark behind. I spoke to Janet

Fisher, the events coordinator of the Prince Charles, who had some history and encounters with the paranormal to share. Some were stories she has experienced herself and others she had heard from staff members and guests who stayed in the hotel, all of which I was glad to hear.

Very shortly after its construction the Prince Charles hosted a wedding (something it has done many times since). It should have been a very happy occasion for all concerned, but it did not end up working out that way. The bride's name was Charlotte and she must have been excited to be married to the man she really loved. Shortly after being married she decided to check on her new husband and went to their room, 701. Sadly she was in the right place, but definitely at the wrong time because, instead of finding her loving husband waiting for her, she saw something that destroyed her body and soul — her new husband in bed with one of her bridesmaids. We can only imagine what was said between the three, but I'm sure it was not pretty. Whatever the verbal exchange was, what happened next is well-known: Charlotte, in a fit of depression, jumped to her death from the eighth floor balcony.

Since her death the eighth floor of the hotel has had more than a few complaints from people hearing a woman crying out in the hallway only to not find anyone out there. Cold spots are a common occurrence all over the floor, as is hearing the sound of a faint woman's voice talking near people's doors when there is no visible or identifiable source for it.

One particular occurrence that Charlotte has picked up in the last few decades is taking a ride on the elevator to the eighth floor. Once in a while one of the elevators will take off without any visible passengers on it — it will go to the eighth floor to deposit its phantom passenger. Janet says this will happen with the most frequency whenever a wedding is being held in the historic hotel... Charlotte is possibly going to check that the groom remains faithful to his vows.

She has been known to appear in guest rooms from time to time. One particular guest awoke to what he thought was his wife standing in the corner of the room. He was shocked to realize she was still asleep next to him; he looked back over toward the woman's figure. It was still barely visible, but very quickly began to fade. He was positive that what he saw was not a trick of a sleepy mind, but that there was a woman in a wedding dress standing in the murky darkness of his room. He also pointed out the room was very cold, which was the whole reason he woke from his sleep in the first place.

Others have seen her as well, from the corner of their eyes or walking down the hall. She has, while not being seen, simply sat on the foot of a bed or given someone a tap or squeeze on the arm.

Janet informed me that Charlotte is not the only spirit that still lingers in the elegant hotel; there is also the ghost of a Cumberland County

Chief of Police who died in a fourth floor room. I was able to speak to Mr. Bruce Dawes, who is a Cumberland County historian, about this. He was able to inform me that not only was this a documented murder, but that it happened in the late 1920s and that the Chief of Police's name was Jay Ross Jones. Mr. Jones had checked himself into a room on the fourth floor in the Prince Charles; it was later in the evening when several guests he had invited to his room found him with a gunshot to the left temple of his head. It was later discovered that the gun used to shoot him was his very own .45.

Many believed that, like the bride before him, he took his own life; others say he was killed by someone with an axe to grind against the officer of the law. If he was murdered, his killer was never found and his death went unanswered for, which may explain why he has stuck around. The former chief of police has reportedly been a constant presence on the fourth floor since the 1930s and has shown no signs of stopping in the last few years.

He is not centered on any one room on the fourth floor, as people often claim to feel as if someone is in their rooms with them or report problems with lights and other electronics. One room in particular has had several air-conditioners break without any reason. Water faucets will cut on and off by themselves. Others hear what sounds like a heavy-footed man stomping around in the room or, sometimes, out in the hall.

Janet had her own paranormal experience on the fourth floor. At the time the entire floor was vacant, she heard the sound of someone walking in the hall. It was extremely loud and she heard it walk toward a room, so she went to see if anybody was on the floor with her. She saw no one in the hall and no signs of anyone having been there, so she walked toward the room. To her surprise, she heard the footsteps approaching her.

She found that the door was still shut, but she could hear something through the door that sounded like running water. At this point she knew for a fact the floor was empty of guests and that no cleaning staff was there at the time. She entered the room to check and see what was going on, expecting to find someone in the room, but instead she found it dark and empty. However, she noticed the faucet in the bathroom was running at full stream.

A former executive chef of the Prince Charles, Keith Kurzeja has heard countless ghost stories during his time at the hotel, but never really put much faith in them being true. One evening in 1994, while blessed with some free extra time, he decided to hang out on the fourth floor and see if any ghosts decided to show themselves. He spent nearly a half-hour on the floor and saw nothing of any paranormal nature; he figured this was proof that the floor had no ghostly guest and turned to get on the elevator and head to the bottom floor. As soon as his back was turned, Keith got a rude surprise — a swift kick to his behind, which was powerful enough to move him a few inches! He turned around to see who the wise-guy was...only to find the hallway as empty as it was when he first turned around. Keith felt like he got his answer about the ghost on the fourth floor after that.

The housekeeping staff of the Prince Charles has encountered more of the paranormal than anyone else who works in the hotel. It is while doing their cleaning duties that they will often encounter some kind of paranormal phenomenon. One of the resident spirits will shut the room doors while they are cleaning, and, like Janet Fisher, many members of the housekeeping staff will hear heavy walking in the hallway only to find no one when they check to see who it is. This has been said to happen on a few floors, making it hard to say which one of the ghosts it is, but a good guess by the heavy walking would lean toward a male specter.

A strictly fourth floor incident is that of a male voice talking too low to understand what he is saying, but loud enough to be heard by those nearby. It is normally while they are in empty rooms as they are cleaning that the sound of this phantom man can be heard. Most people who hear it often check to see if they have the TV on or maybe coming from another room. The TV will be off and when they leave the room to see if the sound is also in the hallway they hear nothing coming from any of the rooms. Then the voice will stop entirely only to heard again whenever he decides to speak up again.

Over the decades the Prince Charles has had its share of unexplained phenomenon. Still those who seem to be haunting it have never been cause for alarm; they are pleasant enough and don't seem to want to scare anyone. They give people something to talk about when their vacations or shifts are over. After all, everyone loves a good ghost story.

The Kyle House

A prestigious boy's academy used to sit where the Kyle House does today, but in 1831 the great fire of Fayetteville destroyed six hundred buildings, including the boy's academy. It would be many years later that a man named James Kyle bought the land and began constructing his home on the site. Learning from the fire that he had lost property in as well, he had the walls built eighteen inches thick and filled with sand and homemade bricks to deter any future fires.

James Kyle was well-known in the Fayetteville community. An immigrant from Scotland who had made a tidy fortune as a merchant, he was also a very well respected city figure in his day and often looked to for advice by residents of Fayetteville from issues of politics and economy. He was a source of wisdom for all those who asked for it.

After his death, his daughter, Anne, was the first of his decedents to take over the family home, which she, in turn, handed to her kids (and so on), but in recent years the house was given to St. John's Episcopal Church, which has lovingly cared for it.

Reports of ghosts or, more likely, a single ghost have been heard in the home for decades and there seems to be a firm belief that it is James Kyle making sure his family home is always well respected and treated right by whoever enters it. He has been known to startle those who visit the place by moving objects or brushing by them in empty hallways. He seems to use as many tricks as he can to let people know he is still around.

One particular young lady who had multiple visits to the home knows all about them. Heather Bosher has lived in Fayetteville her entire life and she met most of her lifelong friends there. Even her husband, Shad, is a Fayetteville native. She knows the city like the back of her hand. She also knows many other longtime Fayetteville residents like the Kyle family themselves. Heather has not only been to the Kyle house many times, but is friends with many of the family members.

On almost every one of her visits, unsettling things would occur in the home that no one could seem to explain. She was more than kind to share a few of her encounters with me. When she was younger, members of the Kyle family would often invite her into the historic home. At the time Heather attended St. Johns next door and would often enjoy a visit to the house after services on Sundays.

There was the wondrous feeling of being in such a historic home, but Heather said there was always something else in the home...something less to do with the history and more to do with an ethereal set of eyes on her. She said most of the activity happened on the second floor of the home; if ever they went upstairs they would make sure every door was fully closed and make sure any doors they opened were shut tight when they left. Quite frequently, they would come back to find all the doors on the second floor not just unlocked but wide open. It would seem that someone does not like his or her doors being shut or locked.

It would often seem that James is a heavy-footed man. Heather, along with many others, would hear him walking the upstairs even when they knew there was not another living soul in the home. Sometimes the ethereal Mr. Kyle would also descend the staircase, possibly to join Heather and her friends in conversation. They never gave him a chance to, usually deciding to leave when they heard him coming. Still people have heard what sounded like a man talking too low to understand, but loud enough to be heard all over the house.

Like many haunted locations, the house has its fair share of cold spots, again mainly found on the second floor of the home or on the stairs.

Visitors to the house these days are much fewer in number and most of them do not report too many odd happenings. Possibly James likes the care its current owners put into his house and is giving them a wide berth, as no one likes a backseat caretaker.

The Bentonville Battleground

If the theory that hauntings are normally caused by emotional trauma and distress is accurate, then the battlegrounds of Bentonville would be a prime site for a whopper of one. Imagine going up against a numerically superior army, fighting for what you believe is right and what you must know in your gut is already a lost cause. The fear, anger, and death that would follow would be one of the last great offensive efforts you could wage and you knew a lot rested on your shoulders. Talk about pressure. Such a thing would most likely leave a few lost souls behind who may not want to admit the battle they laid their lives down for was over.

Right outside of Four Oaks, North Carolina, is the historic Bentonville battleground. It is where the last full-scale tactical offensive against the Union was launched by the Confederate army. It was March 19, 1865 and General Sherman was burning his way through the South in order to break what remained of the Confederates' spirit. Joseph E. Johnston, a general in the Confederate Army, was planning to launch an offensive against Sherman to stop his devastating march. To those who know the history of the Civil War, it is well-known that by this point the Confederate cause was more or less a lost one; with supplies depleted, massive territory lost, and ever-growing casualties, to say that emotions were running high within Johnston's men would not be a stretch. Those angry and scared soldiers were about to give the last full measure any man can.

Johnston pit his 16,000 infantry and 4,000 cavalry against Sherman's 60,000 ground forces, which seemed to be symbolic of the main problem the Confederate Army suffered through the entire war — inferior numbers to the Union. Both sides fought bravely between March 19-21, 1865, but when all was said and done the Confederate army retreated via the Mill Creek Bridge, which they burned to prevent Sherman from giving pursuit.

The Battle at Bentonville was over before it began. The defeat was not Johnston's fault. He was even respected by his adversary Sherman, who once said of Johnston, "No officer or solider who ever served under me will question the generalship of Joseph E. Johnson. His retreats were timely, in good order, and left nothing behind."

The direct effect of the Confederate loss was that Sherman and his army were able to seize and occupy Goldsboro for two weeks. There were no more significant attempts to stop or even impede Sherman after the failure at Bentonville and little over a month later at Bennett Place Johnston surrendered to Sherman. This, along with Robert E. Lee's surrender to Grant only a little earlier, meant all the major Confederate forces were out of the picture and the American Civil War was ended.

The site where the battle took place was declared a national historic landmark in 1996 and is now the place of historic reenactments in which the battle is relived to educate today's generation about history and help them live it as well. It always seems that places where reenactments take place stir up a few spirits. In fact some of the most interesting encounters with the paranormal you hear about are often reported by re-enactors.

The battlefield looks pristine these days and even with the historic artifacts around, it is hard to imagine the violence and loss of life that took place there. The care put into preserving the historic feel of the grounds and the Harper House, along with the knowledge of the site that is on hand, really help people get a feel of the three-day battle that made Bentonville a part of American and North Carolina's history, but some say that is not all that keeps the history of the site alive. Have all those who died there found the eternal rest they deserve? It would seem not, as visitors to the park for over a hundred years have encountered Civil War soldiers from both sides still fighting the actual battle!

Could the historic site still have some spirits lurking around? Most battlefields, especially those of the Civil War era, have a few ghost stories attached to them and Bentonville has more than its share. There have been reports of phantom marching and the sounds of battle and encounters with men in full Confederate or Union military attire who simply vanish from sight.

As I said earlier, re-enactors often have some of the best paranormal stories to share. Maybe the lost spirits see the battle happening again and get a little riled up. During the evening hours, when all the battle reenactments had ended for the day, a re-enactor, who was still on the premises admiring the natural scenery, heard what he described as the sound of cavalry charging down the road. He looked around to see if someone was messing around with the horses, but there was nobody out and about on foot, let alone on horseback.

Along the same path people have heard the sound of a large body of people marching, as if an army was moving into position. The problem is that during these times the path and the surrounding area is completely empty. More than one eyewitness has seen soldiers walking in full Confederate military uniform; naturally, people assume that these soldiers are merely re-enactors at first, but then they start to notice how "detailed" their look is: unkempt facial hair on pale and often sunken faces. The uniforms often look ragged, like they have been worn nonstop for years. All these things point to a real Civil War solider and those who see them are even more baffled by the fact no reenactments are being performed at the time.

The sounds are not the only disembodied phenomenon that happens at the battlefield. There is also a collection of strange smells people have noticed. The most commonly reported odor is not a pleasant one. It is described as the smell of decomposing bodies, not something easily missed and no doubt what the field would have smelt like by the third day of the battle. The dead on both sides left lying in the sun would not have been pleasant. Other smells are that of gunpowder, which is sometimes accompanied by the phantom sounds of battle. Severe temperature drops are also noticed all around the site.

Not all of the activity is located on the field though; some of the hauntings happened in the Harper House that is part of the historic site. In 1865, the Harper House belonged to John and Amy Harper, who lived in the house with six of their children. During the Bentonville battle, the house was seized by the Union and used as a field hospital; the family moved into the attic during this period and tried to ignore the fact that wounded and dying men were in and around their home. Civil War field hospitals were almost always scenes of horror; no modern medicine or way to kill the pain (unless you count a swig of whiskey) and the common procedure for any wound to a limb was amputation. Needless to say, a doctor with a saw on his side could be scarier than an enemy solider with a gun. So if the field of battle picked up a few restless spirits from those who died, then it is very possible that the Harper house could have done the same.

Michelle Myers, of the website ghosthuntingsecrets.com, did interviews with re-enactors at the battlefield and came across Brenda McKean, who has spent a lot of time at the battlefield over the years and agreed to share an event that took place while she was on the property a few years earlier.

Brenda witnessed a very interesting sight in front of the house that she is pretty sure was paranormal in nature. She was in the Harper home with several other people and had to go use the toiletries; the only modern facilities were outside, a short distance and a quick walk away. As she was leaving the main house, she noticed a large bonfire in the front yard with another one a small distance off, but thought that it was being done by other re-enactors or park employees. She was fairly certain that fires of any size were not allowed near the Harper home simply because it was an old wooden structure and could easily go up like a book of matches.

When she was leaving the restroom and began heading back inside, she looked back towards the direction of the fires and noticed they had both disappeared in a matter of minutes. She did not hear anyone or see any signs of a smoldering fire and did not smell anything to identify a recently extinguished fire, which should have certainly been there. Nevertheless, she went about her business and when morning came around she checked the area that the fire nearest the house would have been and did not find any signs of ashes or scorched earth — there was no sign of a fire at all. She found a young man who was also part of the reenactment team that had slept in a tent by the Harper House that night, thinking that maybe he knew something about the bonfire. Strangely, the young man informed her that he had nothing to do with any fires the night before and had not seen any sign of a fire.

If the bonfire was paranormal in nature, it could have been from the days during the battle, but the fact they appeared so close to the house makes me think they are linked to the time the Harper House served as a field hospital. As I stated earlier, a wound to any limb could very likely only be taken care of with an amputation, which could cause an excess of dismembered arms and legs that had to be taken care of. The most common way to deal with the amputated limbs was to burn them in large fires, which was most likely done at the Harper house during those turbulent days.

The Harper House seems to be home to some nonmilitary ghosts. A particular gentleman seen in the home is thought to be the ghost of John Harper. He is seen in simple period rustic clothing, but generally for only a few seconds or just out of the corner of someone's eye. Another report linked to him is the sound of a deep-voiced man talking, usually located in the second floor; the talker can never be found and is never clearly understood. It is possible that Mr. Harper has stuck around for some personal reason or, like a lot of the activity on the battlefield, this may be a case of a residual haunting — it's not really his spirit, but only a moment caught in time.

The Bentonville Battleground seems to have a multitude of spirits and phenomena that occur in different times and strength and are witnessed by a large variety of people. As for the staff, it is their express desire that the historic importance of the site be appreciated and that anyone who visits the site remember all those who died there.

Janet Brinkley

Janet Brinkley has, since the day I met her, seemed like there was something special about her. We first met when she got a job at the same deli I worked at. She immediately had a way about her. She seemed to glow with a positive mood and always could tell how I was feeling no matter how I tried to cover it up. Janet is what is commonly referred to as a sensitive; she is more attuned to picking up the spirit world than the average person — something she was forced to figure out at an early age.

Janet does not do "channeling" for people and is generally not in control of who comes to see her. She tries to live a normal life as best she can. She is open to seeing many ghosts — both the good and bad ones. This is where things can get kind of scary for spiritually sensitive people because for every friendly spirit there is generally a negative one! Janet does not let her ability to see the spirits control her life. She lives a perfectly normal one and only sees spirits every so often these days, but her earlier years are full of some fascinating encounters.

She had an interesting childhood growing up with this gift. In 1972, when she was only seven years old, Janet lived in a farmhouse in Smithfield. It was a very old home that had been around since the late 1800s. The house had been witness to some of the dark moments in our state's history, which left their mark.

Janet is not the only one in her family with this ability; her sister seemed to see the same things she did, which was a comfort for Janet when she saw disturbing scenes. It helped her deal with it when she found out that she was not the only one seeing those things.

In front of their house was a very large and old tree with ugly, gnarled branches and a hideous trunk. The tree was enough to give anyone the creeps. It had a dark past of its own. Now and then, it had been used to unjustly hang local blacks in the darker days of the state. According to Janet and her sister, some part of those poor people still lingered after their tragic deaths. They often saw the lifeless body of a black man hanging from the tree. It sent no message and did not interact with them; the body just stayed there, motionless, as he must have looked only moments after his death. He was dressed in ragged clothing from the pre-Civil War era, but it is anyone's guess why and when the horrible crime was committed that caused this particular upsetting sight. Janet saw the poor man hanging from the tree at least once a week the entire time she lived in that house. To this day she still remembers it and the sadness it brought her.

Another spirit that Janet saw was that of a slave woman. Janet noticed her first, but the spirit is more clearly remembered by her sister. The ghost would stand by the old dumbwaiter in the house. She seemed to be cleaning sometimes or preparing a meal and always seemed to have her mind on what she was doing. She was dressed in a long dress that seemed to be from the early to mid-1800s. She was completely unaware of Janet and the rest of the family, either refusing to acknowledge her death or blocking out the modern world around her. Who is to say why this woman was trapped in that moment in time? Maybe she suffered a tragedy shortly before or after it, and maybe she did those chores so often that is all she can remember how to do.

Not all the spirits Janet encountered were so tragic; in fact she seemed to have a guardian angel of sorts. It was a hot summer day when Janet first met her; she was sitting in the rocking chair on the front porch, simply rocking with a smile and humming. She was an older woman, dressed in what Janet described as country attire from the 1930s, and Janet always did her best to avoid her. Like all the other things she seemed to see, if it was not noticed by anyone but her and her sister, she felt she should try to ignore it. Still her parents noticed the chair softly rocking when it appeared to be empty. The woman had a constant presence on the porch and seemed to be completely aware of the current residents of the house, often smiling or waving at Janet as she ran in her home. If the fact she never seemed to leave was not bad enough, the rocking chair she rocked in was right outside Janet's bedroom window. It was while lying in her bed one night that she found out why the woman was there all the time.

Janet lay in her bed and could hear the rocking chair rocking. She was trying her hardest to ignore it when she noticed the sweet old country woman through her bedroom window. She said to Janet, "Don't be afraid dear, I am here to protect you." Janet did not really know how to take what the woman had said; she just tried to get some sleep that night. After that, Janet felt a lot better about this particular spirit. It felt good to know that someone was watching out for her. Her guardian stayed at her perch by Janet's window for the rest of her time in the house. She did not know how much she had done for her until after she lost her.

It 1979, when she was thirteen years old, her family moved to the Russell house, which was also in Smithfield. None of the spirits from the former house followed them — not even Janet's guardian that had been by her side for years at that point. Still Janet and her sister were not given a reprieve from their sightings by the change of locations; this new home had its own group of spirits they would meet.

The most vocal entity in the home that they saw the most was not a former resident, but a ghost dog. Janet described it as a mixed breed that was small in stature. It was extremely aware of all those around him (or maybe her, who knows) often running up to the girls barking as if it wanted to play with them. Sometimes he would just wander down the hall as if he owned the place. He would disappear for days at a time and come back like he had never been gone; Janet got a kick out of watching him bark at people who could not even see him.

Her second home had a more somber spirit that only appeared sitting on the stairs by the front door. The first time Janet saw her, she thought maybe she was one of the neighbors or possibly one of her mom's friends. The woman was just sitting on the stairs looking down, intensely; she looked completely solid so Janet said hello. This did not earn an acknowledging glance from her, as she still focused on the door. At this time, Janet finally noticed that not only was she wearing a very fancy gown, but also the gown looked like it was from the late nineteenth or early twentieth century. Janet slowly walked in front of her and noticed she still didn't have any of her attention; her eyes remained focused on the door.

Later, Janet found out that at the turn-of-the-century a young woman lived in the house and on one particular evening, she was supposed to go out on a date with a local boy she had fallen in love with. For some reason, he never showed up, though she waited all night for him to come. When she finally gave up, she committed suicide in a moment of extreme emotional agony.

By the time she was thirteen, Janet had witnessed many paranormal beings, but it was the first time she would be truly terrified by one. While lying in her bed light at night, before sleep normally would overcome her, she felt a very uneasy feeling of being watched and hovered over. Overwhelmed by the feeling of someone or something being in the room with her, she lifted her head and turned her view toward the foot of her bed. What she saw was the most horrific sight she could imagine. It was a black mass in the shape of a human body and on the top was a monstrous face. She described it as if it was a decomposed face of a man. Its eyes were black voids and the rest of the face was caved in, with an extremely pale complexion. While it stood there the temperature dropped all around her. It spoke to her in a terrifying voice and warned her, "I will win." Janet did the only thing she could do, which was look away. When she finally looked back, the creature had disappeared. It did not hurt her feelings any that it had taken off.

Janet never forgot this creature that harassed her; she said he even came back a few more times over the years, but she refused to be bullied ever again. Janet still has a strong connection with the unseen around her, but she has learned to live with it, realizing it is part of who she is in this world.

One thing she is positive of is that Smithfield has more earthbound souls than anywhere else she has been in the state of North Carolina.

Chapter Four

Coastal Tidewater

The Battleship North Carolina

It is hard to miss the 728-foot ship as you enter Wilmington, North Carolina. The *Battleship North Carolina* is a piece of American history from a bygone naval era, a time before precision weaponry or computerized targeting. The days of the battleships became numbered as soon as jet engines made it possible for an aircraft carrier to be more destructive than any battleship could ever be. Though it's been over sixty years since the *North Carolina* was used for any naval missions, she is still a proud symbol of the state it carries the name of as a living piece of history.

I have lived in Wilmington for over six years, but the first time I saw the battleship was over a decade ago. I have been back more times I can count since. From the moment I set foot on the deck I am always overwhelmed by the feeling of being on a piece of history like the *North Carolina*. It is not hard to lose yourself in the history, to look over the side of the ship and see the Pacific Ocean instead of the Wilmington cityscape, and to imagine the sailors and naval personnel doing their duties on deck instead of tourists taking pictures and to wonder what it would be like on the ship as it fought in any one of its many engagements during the war. Then I take a moment to be amazed at how, despite a few close calls over the years, she survived the course of the Second World War when many did not.

It is not a stretch to think that a vessel that was built with war and by extension death in mind could possibly be home to a few restless spirits. Any location during war can be a hotbed of countless emotions (anger, fear, and sadness) and all of this can leave savage, ugly marks on the environment around it. Before going into the ghost onboard, it is very important to have the proper respect and understanding of the *North Carolina* and her history before trying to think about why or who may be haunting the old girl.

Battleship North Carolina.

By 1937 a lot was going on around the globe: the Depression was still in full swing, leaving over one-third of the American population without work; the Third Reich was gearing up for war; and Japan was hostilely acquiring territories all over Asia in hopes of becoming a self-sufficient empire. America had depleted its naval power after World War I and had not produced a new battleship in two decades. Still, even with America's hope to remain neutral in the increasing likelihood of war, President Roosevelt was trying to create new jobs for Depression-ravaged Americans and, as the saying goes, it is better to be safe than sorry and the decision to construct new naval vessels was made.

On August 1, 1937, the order for the construction of the *Battleship North Carolina* was sent to the New York Naval Yards and soon a myriad of hardy construction workers and welders began the task of making the blueprints into literal and physical reality. In the nearly three years it took to construct the ship, the inevitable war became reality. On September 1, 1939, Nazi-led Germany invaded Poland and the Second World War started as the Allied nations declared war on the Axis powers in response to the invasion. Even while the world was starting a struggle between liberty and tyranny, the United States remained out of the war. The *North Carolina* was launched June 13, 1940, and was the first of the navy's new heavily armored 16-inch gun fleet to be completed.

The Navy was more than happy to show off their new acquisition, so much in fact that the *North Carolina* soon became known as the "showboat" — she was displayed at naval bases across the country. On December 7, 1941, the Empire of Japan attacked the American Naval yards at Pearl Harbor and by December 8th the United States declared war on Japan, bringing an end to any hope the United States had of staying out of the war.

The *North Carolina* served in all major Naval conflicts in the Pacific theater, where she performed her primary duty of protecting aircraft carriers (ironically the vessel that made battleships obsolete). During her time in World War Two, ten of *Battleship North Carolina's* crew were killed, five in just one torpedo attack. Despite the damage she took and the crew that were lost, she stayed in through the entire duration of the Pacific theater, serving her nation with pride and strength.

The *North Carolina* was no longer needed after VJ-day (Victory over Japan) and soon found that she was without a purpose. The ship was decommissioned in New York on June 27, 1947, nearly a decade after the order of its construction was given. Eventually she was stricken from the Naval Vessel registry, which meant the once-proud ship could have been stripped down for scrap metal like many other ships had been before.

Luckily for the ship (and all the history buffs out there), the people of the state of North Carolina stepped in to save it. It took $330,000 (one-third of which was raised by school children) to have the ship transferred over to the state and, on September 6, 1961, the *North Carolina* came to her new home in Wilmington.

It was on one of my many visits to the ship that I first learned of the paranormal activity that occurred onboard. It was a breathtaking summer day in 2000; the sun was beating down and the air had the faint taste of salt that I always notice when I am near the ocean. The ship was overflowing with families on vacation from across the country and I was heading into the interior of the ship. It only deepens my respect for those who served on the *North Carolina* when I am clumsily trying to navigate the narrow corridors filled with people, as I can only imagine how it would have been during a battle.

I had already visited the galley and was leaving the bunk area, thinking I had seen all there was to see in that area. Had I stayed just a few minutes longer I may have been able to see firsthand what I am about to relate. I was only a little bit away from the bunk room when I started hearing a lot of talking and excited chatter coming from inside there, so I decided to see what the reason for the commotion was. Quickly, I returned to the room to find at least ten people around one bunk talking about what just happened.

I gathered what had happened from several people in the bunk room, visitors who were taking photos and looking around. It was while looking at the bunks that someone noticed an indent on the springs at the foot of the bed, like someone was sitting on it. This immediately started them gasping. People were generally confused and, while they were still staring at the bunk, the imprint changed into the shape of a man laying on the bed! Everybody was at a loss for a rational explanation for what they were seeing. It only lasted a matter of moments and then it seemed the phantom sleeper just vanished. Even though I missed seeing it for myself that day, I was able to hear the firsthand accounts only moments after the activity stopped, allowing me to hear the story in its truest form.

It was very shortly after its arrival in North Carolina that the first odd reports started coming in. After the ship closed down for the night, members of the staff would often hear the sounds of people talking on the ship though everyone had left and, while on the ship, people would hear someone whispering right behind them, only to turn around and find no one there.

Andrew Whitley has been a part of the battleship's living history department for about five years. He and his fellow re-enactors dress in full World War II naval attire to perform the duties that would have been done during the *North Carolina's* days as a naval vessel, which brings her back to life for people to see. As a result, Andrew and his fellow re-enactors would spend the night on the ship so they would be ready the next day. In September 2008, Andrew would, for his first and only time, have an encounter with one of the ship's spirits near the executive office. Andrew described the area as a compartmentalized corridor. As he worked his way down the passageway, he saw the back of another young man in period clothing turn the corner ahead of him. He was nearly positive he was the only member of the crew in that area. Wondering whom he had just seen, Andrew followed the young man and turned the corridor — only to find the passageway was completely empty. He had been on the ship long enough to know that the way he was walking from was also the only way out of that part of the ship. He was told by another member of the living crew that a ghost of a young man haunted that part of the ship. He is often seen in that very area, quickly maneuvering the corridors as if on a mission.

The night guard, Danny Bradshaw, is, perhaps, the employee with the most encounters of paranormal activity reported on the ship. He has been a proud member of the *North Carolina* staff for over twenty years and received the job through a friend who had held the position for a couple of years before he got it. This friend warned Danny that there were ghosts onboard. Danny was skeptical about it, thinking that whatever his friend had heard or seen there was probably a rational explanation.

As night watchman, Danny was given a room onboard the ship to have a place to relax as well as a base of operations. Danny spent the first ten months without a single encounter with the paranormal, but that all changed late one evening. While in his room relaxing for a bit, he heard someone running in the corridor behind his room. As a security officer, his first thought was that some teenagers had snuck onboard and were up to no good. Danny grabbed his flashlight and went into the corridor and turned the light in the direction the footsteps had been running toward, only to find that he was alone. He found this perplexing enough, but, while standing there trying to make sense of it, the phantom runner ran right by him. He did not see anything; he only *heard* the running and endured the unpleasant sensation of a bitter coldness, like all the heat had been sucked out of the air as it ran by.

Danny remembered what his friend had told him about the ship being haunted and was more inclined to believe him. Still Danny did not really know how to react to this. After all dealing with a haunting was not part of the training procedures for a night watchman, and you can't call the cops on a ghost or tell a spirit it is past business hours.

One of Danny's more interesting encounters he shared with me took place during the winter of 1989. A friend of his was bringing some food she had kindly cooked for his dinner. Danny was going to meet her in the parking lot to save her the trouble of walking to his room, but she arrived before he got there and began to honk her horn to let him know she was there. The funny thing is she kept doing it as if she thought he was not coming. Danny reached her only to find her shocked he was right by her car. She proceeded to inform him that there was someone in his room peering through the porthole, so she had assumed it was him. Danny told her that he was completely alone on the ship, but she got him in her car and then drove back a little until they were parked parallel with his bedroom window. This time the curtains were drawn and the porthole was bare. While sitting there and looking at the window, the phantom face once again pulled back the curtain and began looking out the window. Whoever it was quickly withdrew his head and shut the curtain. Both of them had to assume that if there was no living person aboard the ship at the time, it had to be a ghost, possibly trying to figure out what the commotion outside was.

One of the battleship's resident spirits.

Over the years Danny has seen and heard a lot on the old "showboat." Footsteps, disembodied voices, and a blond-haired apparition that seems to just stare and then vanish are just a few of the things he has witnessed. Danny's most interesting and possibly scariest encounter involves another apparition that is a little more unsettling and is one that absolutely stands out from the rest.

The incident occurred during the summer of 1995, when he was going though the lower decks near the galley to cut off the lights. He had made this very same journey on countless evenings and was sure that he knew everything to expect, but he was not ready for the unbelievably scary sight that greeted him: a man with his head engulfed in white flame! The apparition seemed completely unbothered by his head being on fire and just seemed to be there to let Danny know he was. Like any sane human being, Danny did not stick around to see if he had any other plans; instead, he quickly worked his way towards the deck.

This would not be the only time he saw this particular fiery ghost. It came back in 1997 and like before, he just seemed to want nothing more than to give Danny a startle. Danny kept this one close to the chest because of the very bizarre nature of it, figuring this was something people would have the hardest time believing. He found out from a former coworker that he was not the only one to see this burning headman. His friend told him it had happened many years before while he was on the deck of the ship; his attention was drawn over to the sixteen-inch guns on the deck for some reason and then he saw a man standing there that had a head made of white flame who made no attempt at communication and left him completely unnerved. This was a big relief to Danny to know he was not alone in seeing this particular unnerving ghost.

Why did this particular ghost choose to manifest with his head engulfed in flames? Perhaps he is one of the sailors who lost his life on the ship and possibly suffered fire damage to his face, or maybe he has a whole other reason for his form, but short of him telling someone, there is no way to be certain.

The ghosts on the ship are generally friendly and playful specters that simply cause just enough activity to be acknowledged. Others that bark orders at Danny like "get out of here" might be under the belief that they are still in the throes of World War II and Danny is a face they did not know. Danny now believes that the entities have become comfortable with his presence and may see him as just as much a part of the ship as they are. He still hears from them time to time, just enough to remind him he is not the only person on the battleship during the lonely nights.

If you would like to hear more about Danny's experience on the ship, I encourage you to pick up his book *Ghosts on the Battleship North Carolina*.

The *Battleship North Carolina* is truly a wonder to tour; it is a piece of history that it is an honor to set foot on. She has been a labor of love since her construction when she was a symbol of national strength. Her salvation by the citizens of North Carolina and even to this day as countless people spends so much time and energy keeping her in wonderful condition and making sure people stay interested in her. I encourage everyone to go see it, if only because of the beauty and majesty of this floating museum. Who knows... you might spot one of her old crew still walking the ship.

The Cotton Exchange

Located in Wilmington's historic riverfront is a set of interconnected buildings, the oldest of which has been around since the pre-Civil War era. The Cotton Exchange, as it is called, now houses many stores and restaurants and is a wonderful place to do some shopping. What a joy it is to shop in such an historic setting. The buildings that make it up, since their earliest days, have always existed for the purpose of commerce. The Exchange is divided between eight buildings: the Sprunt, O'Brien, Bear, Wood Seed, Dahn Hardt, Granary, and Nutt buildings and the Front Street entrances. Five of the buildings house the twenty-eight stores and restaurants.

It should come as no surprise that at one point there actually was a cotton exchange in one of the buildings. It existed around 1920 in what is now known as the Sprunt Building. Alexander Sprunt owned and operated The Cotton Exchange and now the entire complex carries on his business name, but, with the exception of cotton clothing, it is no longer actually a cotton exchange.

If you ever get a chance to shop in The Cotton Exchange, it will take you back to another time. If you exit on the Nutt Street side, you are greeted by the riverfront. In another time, paddle ships and oceanic liners would sail down it, loaded with goods and resources from across the country (and even the world), most of which would be headed to the one of the buildings within the complex.

The Exchange has remained, as paddle ships faded away from the river and were replaced by trucks on the road and planes in the air. It has seen the Wilmington cityscape change; new buildings would come and go yet The Exchange has persevered and remained in its original location.

With such a long history The Cotton Exchange is not just home to many places of business, but also to more than just a few folks who are not ready to leave the mortal world. Paranormal activity is not new to The Cotton Exchange. People reporting paranormal encounters go back for decades; the costumers' and storeowners' reports of ghosts have been coming for years. The activity ranges from phantom noises to the holy grail of the paranormal, which is the full-bodied apparition.

I was lucky enough to have some storeowners within The Exchange generously share some of their encounters with me.

You are My Sunshine, a baby clothing and supply store located in the Bear building, is ran by a very pleasant woman whose name is Carmen Cosby. She is one of the shopkeepers who have had her own personal encounter with some of The Exchange's ethereal crowd. She was very gracious to tell me about some of her encounters.

Carmen's store has everything a new mother could need: clothes, supplies, and even dolls to make any child smile. It was a certain set of a boy and girl dolls that produced one of Carmen's first encounters with a spook. There was nothing peculiar about the dolls themselves, a blond girl and a brown-hair boy. The dolls had been on a high shelf on the right side of her store for a while, then one day a customer came through and was so taken by the boy doll that she purchased it. However, she had no interest in the girl doll, so she left it behind at the store.

The sale was made and the blond doll now sat on her shelf by its lonesome. Soon it became apparent that someone was not happy about one of the dolls being sold. The next day, as Carmen was going about her regular work, she was surprised when, with no warning, the remaining doll was hurled from the shelf toward the center of the store! Carmen was positive the doll had traveled too far for it to just have fallen, but there was no one near it at the time and the shelf was too high for most people to reach.

One ghost seemed to really like these dolls.

After the doll had displayed its impressive flying trick another sign of someone being unhappy manifested — a putrid smell arose right from the area that the doll had been tossed from. Carmen noticed the smell right away. She tried to locate a normal cause for it, but could not. She was not the only one who smelled it. Her customers and friends noticed it as well whenever they walked to that side of the store. No one was able to find what was causing the nauseous smell. It only seemed to be affecting that one area of the store. The odor lasted for only a few days and then disappeared without a trace like it had never been there. She never found an answer to what caused it. There were no busted pipes or any other possible causes that could be located, and it appeared to be some sort of aroma based in protest about the selling of the doll.

On another occasion the playful spirit had fun with the store security system. While she was locking up for the evening Carmen was activating her motion detector (or at least trying to). The motion detector was picking someone up in the store so it refused to arm. She double-checked by asking, "Is anyone still here?" No one responded. Thinking that it might be a glitch or something, she went and tried again with the exact same results. She thought maybe the ghost that had chucked her doll was messing with her, so she figured to give it a shot and tell the entity to knock it off. To her great surprise the playful spirit did in fact stop after being told to. She was able to set her system and leave for the evening.

Now who would be so upset by a simple doll being sold? The most likely answer would be a child who was attached to it and Carmen is sure she came face-to-face with this very child. One day, while she had her own bundle of joy in the store with her, Carmen was looking out the store window that peered into the hallway in-between the stores. She noticed a reflection other than her own in the glass...that of a small girl who was looking right at her. She turned around to see who this young lady was, but no one was behind her and no children were in the store at all. She quickly looked back to the window and found that the little girl's reflection was still there — and that is when Carmen noticed that, unlike her reflection, which appeared in multiple glass panels, the child's reflection was only in just the single, solitary pane of glass.

The young girl was a small blond headed child who looked no older than seven. She seemed to be wearing early nineteenth century clothing. The small girl soon vanished entirely from the window, indicating no apparent source of where she came from. She just seemed to be there to take a good, hard look at Carmen and her baby. Who this little girl may have been is not really known, but she seemed to be attached to the baby store. Maybe the little haunter came for all the toys, which is without a doubt, a child's paradise or possibly she came to see the mothers who shop and even work there because maybe, just maybe, they remind her of her own mother. Still, we shall never truly know.

Carmen is positive that this little girl is the one responsible for the majority of the activity in her store. When a little child loses a favorite toy they often throw a pretty big fit, like she did when the doll was sold. Little kids like to be playful, quite like the one Carmen had to deal with while trying to lock up her store, yet also, like a little girl would, respond when ordered by a mother-figure telling her stop.

The little girl seems to be a playful spirit with only mischief and fun on her mind, but she is not the only entity that Carmen has encountered. She only met this particular entity once, but it is one she will likely never be able to forget. It was just a regular day at The Cotton Exchange. The building was filled with customers going from store to store and filling up the corridors between them. Carmen was making casual conversation with some of the customers as they passed by. It was while doing this that she noticed a man bent over like he was trying to pick something up. It seemed like it was taking him longer than it should so Carmen walked toward him to see if he needed a hand. As Carmen drew near him, she noticed he was dressed in odd attire; it was a black suit and pants along with a black hat that looked to be from a much earlier time. Along with this the man just seemed to be radiating an aura that gave her a very bad feeling. She felt uncomfortable as she drew near him. Despite all this she reached toward him to give him a tap on the shoulder and offer her help, but as she was about to make contact he simply vanished before her eyes. No sign of the gentleman was anywhere and no one seemed to have noticed that he vanished without a trace, right before her eyes. Carmen told me this was the only time that any experience she encountered has ever made her uncomfortable. This phantom man has never reappeared to her and she is just fine with that.

It goes without saying that there is a lot more than one haunted location within the shopping complex of the historic Cotton Exchange. Everything from stores, restaurants, and all the places in-between seem to have a ghost show up at least once.

The Basics is a restaurant within The Exchange that seems to have one reoccurring hot spot, which is a staircase located in the back of the establishment. More than one staff member has seen a full-bodied apparition briefly on the stairs over the years. What they have seen seemed to be a young woman dressed in a white gown from the late 1800s. She is transparent; her face is only seen for a brief moment and it never seems to have any features that can be distinguished, but comes across as something more like a vague form made of white mist.

She seems to have a mean streak, which has been proven on at least one occasion with a former member of the wait staff. A young waitress, who was traveling down the back stairs while keeping her mind on her work, received a violent jolt when she was forcibly shoved down the stairs by an unseen force. She received a few minor injuries for her troubles and no explanation as to why she had been pushed. She was very startled by this unprovoked attack and was absolutely positive that she was pushed and had not simply tripped over her own two feet. She claimed to have felt something like a full-grown person ramming into her back, which sent her tumbling down the stairs. Although the entity does not make a habit of this kind of attack, many people who travel those stairs often feel a very uneasy and often startling vibe from it.

A clothing store called The Top Toad is located in the Granary building; among a very wide selection of apparel it also seems to have a selection of a different kind. One of the clerks is a young woman named Alex, and she has seen and heard many stories from her coworkers and the customers in her time there.

Inside the store a specter of a little boy has been seen, well at least part of him anyway. A customer noticed his head while she was checking out at the register. The customer glanced over to the children's department and noticed a small boy's face looking off into the distance. At first she did not think this odd until she noticed his body stopped at the neck. He stood there and never averted his stare from whatever it was he was looking at and then quietly faded away. This phantom's head has only been seen that one time and as far as anyone else knows has never reappeared.

A common specter that has been seen more than once is a friendly and somewhat musical one. A very unassuming elderly man is often seen sitting on the bench right outside the store, normally humming to himself. He appears very solid and would just seem like a customer taking a rest if it was not for the fact he vanishes without a trace in a matter of seconds — who he was and why he seems to have the need to hum is not known, but he seems to be a welcomed entity that simply wants to sit and watch the customers walk by and provide a little music to those listening.

Much like Carmen's store, Top Toad had an incident that involved the store's security system being messed with. The store security camera's monitor, for some unknown reason, continuously displayed green bars going through it and the pictures were distorted. The staff checked everything they could think of to make sure it was not a technical problem and found everything to be fine. The monitor kept displaying the bizarre images on screen. After ruling out all the possible explanations except the ghost one, they decided to tell the spirits to restore the video to its normal quality and stop messing around; in a matter of seconds the image went back to its normal appearance.

At least one of the store's "haunts" is pretty sensitive to what is said about them, which was proven one evening after closing. One of the store's employees had come late one night, along with her boyfriend, to pick up her paycheck. She was nervous about being in the store so late at night. When she told her boyfriend her nervous demeanor was because of the ghost, he thought the very concept was outrageous and laughed as loud as he could about it and poked fun at her. The couple left the store and she did not think twice about the whole thing until her shift started the next day. Upon entering the hallway leading to the Top Toad she saw something that did not seem quite right. All the clothes that normally hang on the walls outside the store were no longer hanging up, but, as she walked into work, she noticed that they seemed to be gone.

She was informed when she went in and talked to her fellow employees who were already there that the clothes in the hall had all been tossed off the walls. This occurred when the door to that part of The Exchange had been padlocked shut and the building was empty of any living person. The first people to start work that day found the clothes scattered all over the floor. It was as if someone had thrown a temper tantrum and took it out on the merchandise. All of the products were accounted for and there were no signs of someone attempting a forcible entry, so, to the general populace, the motive was a mystery. Yet to this young employee, who had been there with her boyfriend the night before, there was no doubt that this was simply a message that screamed: "I don't like being laughed at!"

All across the Exchange activity abounds. A ghostly laugh has been heard by several folks in The Exchange coming from one of the women's bathroom. When people work up the courage to go inspect the cause of the creepy laugh, they, to their extreme bewilderment, always find nothing; nobody and nothing earthly is ever found that could explain the laughing. On the outside of the Dahn Hardt building The Celtic Shop has had the bell above its door ring as if someone was entering the store without so much a movement from the door.

In the O'Brien building there are at least two distinct military specters that have been reported. One is a Revolution era solider. Even though the building was built many decades after the War for Independence, it is not a farfetched assumption that a few soldiers lost their lives in the vicinity where The Cotton Exchange now sits and (if you are willing to believe in the existence of paranormal beings and activity) decided to remain attached to the location where he was, even as the structure was built around him.

At one point a local sensitive was invited by one of merchants to try and find out some information about the ghost. She met the solider, and "he" made it clear to the psychic that he was very aware of his physical death and stayed behind because he wanted "people to know his sorrowful plight."

As I mentioned earlier, this is not the only military specter on-site. The second one is from another famous conflict. A ghost of a Civil War solider has been seen standing in one of the stores in the O'Brien building. He is always described as wearing a blue uniform, which would almost definitely mean he was a Union solider. Besides being seen neither of these military men have been linked to any paranormal activity in the building.

The majority of The Exchange's ethereal residents seem to be, more or less, playful and exhibit only the occasional direct contact with the living. Most of the storeowners who have encountered the spirits believe that they, once living beings themselves, should be respected and not treated like sideshow attractions. If they show up, it should be treasured, but people should not goad them into making an appearance. After all, if one of them wants you to see them, it seems they can do it anytime they choose. Regardless of why the ghosts are there, they are there for the long haul and that is just fine with the people of The Cotton Exchange.

Maco Lights

The Maco lights were last seen in 1977, so why include it in this book you may ask. Well the main reason is this is a ghost story that even a President of the United States took interest in.

The most commonly believed origin of the Maco lights was the tragedy of Joe Baldwin, a man killed in a horrific train accident in 1867. The story goes like this: Joe Baldwin had dozed off on the caboose of a train on the old Wilmington-Manchester-Augusta Line. Joe snapped back to life when he realized the caboose he was riding in was slowing down. He ran to the front of the car and noticed it had been detached from the rest of the train and was now gliding to a stop. Joe was hit by a dreadful realization when he saw another train approaching from behind. Deciding not to save himself but rather the lives of those on the approaching train, Joe grabbed a lantern from the end of the train and began waving it back frantically to signal his location to the oncoming train. Sadly he did not succeed — his car was destroyed by the train collision. People who witnessed it said that Joe kept waving his lantern all the way up till the train wreck. The force of the impact reportedly decapitated Joe Baldwin; his lantern was tossed into the nearby wooded area.

At the time that area was called Farmers Turnout; it remained an important train route long after the accident occurred. Still it was not exactly the same after Joe's tragic accident and soon something new began showing up on the tracks — a ghostly light was seen waving frantically off in the distance down the rail. It first showed up only a matter of days after Joe's death, so people became convinced it was Joe's ghost still trying to signal oncoming trains to stop.

Regardless of what caused them, the light soon caused a very real problem for trains coming down the track. Trains were equipped with emergency lights in case they ever became stranded on a track and needed to let other trains know to slow down to avoid an accident (not unlike Joe's). Well on multiple occasions the ghost light at Farmers Turnout was mistaken for just such a signal, causing trains to stop in a hurry to avoid what they thought could be a tragedy. Imagine their surprise when there was no train on the tracks or anything for that matter. Needless to say, the light was always gone with no sign of who or what caused it. This mistaken light could possibly lead to horrible train wrecks so the people at Farmers Turnout were quick to act on this problem: all trains were ordered to have both red and green emergency lights to avoid further confusion with Joe's ghost light.

Here is where the president part comes in. It was the year 1889 and President Grover Cleveland's Presidential Train made a stop at Farmers Turnout. While he was there he noticed the green lights on the trains. Never having seen this kind of lighting system at any other train station before this, President Cleveland was compelled to ask one of the nearby crew at the station the reason for the two colored lights. The man was more than happy to tell the President all about Joe Baldwin's death and his ghostly light that haunted the track and caused all the problems for oncoming trains.

President Grover Cleveland hears of Joe Baldwin's sad fate.

President Cleveland was fascinated by the story and the phenomenon connected to it. He took the mysterious supernatural story with him when he returned to Washington. His fascination soon caused national attention to be shown on the once just-Wilmington-local-oddity. Very shortly after his return to Washington, President Cleveland had a research expedition sent back to the Farmers Turnout to round up some answers. They ended up deciding it was caused by nearby natural gases; however, even with this claim many decades later the Smithsonian sent its own team to study the lights and Fort Bragg actually sent a machine gun detachment to figure out the cause of the lights. Also over the decades parapsychologists have flocked to the famous light's location at Maco Station trying to test their own ideas. The theories were many, but no concrete evidence to back any of the theories and tests was ever delivered.

To all those who assume the Joe Baldwin explanation is forgotten, they should consider this fact: as I mentioned the lights stopped in 1977, which coincided with the removal of the very section of track that the light hovered around. It should at least leave one to wonder why a simple removal of train tracks would cause the centuries-old phenomenon to finally stop. Maybe Joe's ghost finally felt with the track gone the danger was over.

Orton's

Downtown Wilmington has a wide selection of bars to choose from for all tastes. These places have every kind of spirits a person on the town can imagine: margaritas, bourbon, beer, and some even have a few of the ethereal ones.

We all know what a barfly is and chances are, we know a few people that fall into such a category. They are those people so dedicated to their favorite watering hole that they never want to leave it. Imagine someone who does not just spend the whole day there, but the night too, and not just for a week or a year. How about six decades! Fat Tony's Bar and Orton's Pool Hall have a group of formerly living individuals who have stuck around long after they cashed in the check on their earthly lives.

Actually those that haunt the bar and pool hall are not former customers of those particular establishments, but rather the five-story hotel that used to stand in that location. Orton's Hotel was a well-known hotel in early part of the twentieth century until, in the year 1949, during the bitter cold that came with the month of January, a street cop on his regular patrol in downtown Wilmington noticed a fire at the hotel. The officer quickly went for help.

Soon firemen and police arrived and were in full force trying to subdue the growing flames that swallowed the hotel. By 4:30 in the morning the fire was successfully put out. At first it appeared all the guests and staff had been safely evacuated. Everyone breathed a little easier for a short time, but sadly their belief turned out to be incorrect because there were two people still in the hotel as it burned that fateful evening. An elderly gentleman by the name of J. R. Mallard, who was in town visiting his sick brother, never made it out of the hotel. His body was discovered twenty-seven days after the fire. Along with him was a young man by the name of William Stephen, whose whole body was never found; only parts of him that were later identified.

Why these two men did not make it out is unclear. It was reported that other guests saw an elderly gentleman believed to be Mallard wandering around in the smoke in some kind of daze. Most likely the late hour combined with the surrounding panic and his advanced age of seventy put him in a confused state and unable to figure out what was going on. He very likely died from smoke inhalation.

As for William Stephen, there is no way to know for sure why he did not leave the hotel in the panic. It's possible he simply slept through the commotion until it was too late, but that is just a hypothesis; no one knows for sure.

In the end, the popular hotel was laid to waste, with only one exception — the pool hall that was in the basement survived with relatively little damage. The pool hall now lives on as Orton's Bar and Pool Hall. Orton's is very popular and is often filled with locals, college students, and tourists trying to unwind after a hard day of work, sightseeing, or classes, but there are claims of other folk who hang around — those of the people who died in the fire all those years ago.

The staff and crowds at Orton's have seen and heard many unusual things during the evening hours. Odd thuds and sounds that resemble someone's footsteps have been heard in the back of the room, even when there is no one there. People hear low voices talking around them while they are alone. The most common phenomenon that is reported is that of shadowy figures that darts back and forth. They have been seen everywhere in the Orton's: near the pool table, at the bar, even in the bathrooms.

Orton's has old subterranean tunnels left from its days as a hotel that have long been abandoned, which they sometimes let people explore. They often do tours on Halloween for all those who dare to take them. It was Halloween of 2008 when a young woman named Maria had a strange occurrence while she was taking the tour of those tunnels. She, along with a multitude of others, had entered the dark tunnel. With no electricity to provide overhead lighting, they were forced to rely on flashlights. People where snapping pictures all around her when, all of the sudden, every single one of the flashlights died at the exact same time, along with many people's cameras. This caused a lot of commotion and they soon exited the tunnels.

As soon as they left the tunnels, the power returned to the devices like it had never happened. This by itself was odd, but it was later that evening while some folks were reviewing their photos that some people noticed the photos they took right before the equipment went dead had a multitude of "orbs" in them. Any paranormal investigator will tell you that there is a hundred and one ways to end up with orbs in a photo; dust in the air or light reflection to name a few, but what makes this unique was in the pictures taken all the way to a few seconds before the blackout no orbs appeared at all.

In 2008, a local paranormal investigation group known as the Carolina Supernatural Phenomena Observation Team (CSPOT) performed an in depth investigation of Orton's. They came to the local nightspot with everything they had — cameras, EMF detectors, audio recorders, and video — and were fully ready for anything and everything they could possibly encounter.

They did not have any trouble encountering signs of the paranormal as their investigation got under way. Matt, one of the cofounders of CSPOT, was more than happy to share their findings with me.

They performed their investigation during the night after Orton's had closed up until the next day. They spent some time in every part of the establishment, including the bathrooms where people had reported some activity, and they encountered something themselves. On the floor of the bathroom was a large shapeless black mass. The team could tell right away that this was no shadow or trick of the eye; it was something else entirely. It took off rather quickly as the team tried to approach it to get a better look.

In the back of Orton's another group of the team was heading closer to the back of the bar when, out of nowhere, another black object flew though the air right past them. As luck would have it they were recording as they walked and were able to catch the object on film.

The part they were most eager to explore, which some say is the area with the most activity, was the old tunnels behind the pool hall, as this has been the setting for many unearthly encounters. During their time there multiple team members reported odd and unexplainable noises coming from the tunnels.

CSPOT's investigation also procured some very interesting EVPs that they are pretty sure helped nail down a few of the spirits in the bar. A little girl's voice was caught several times; she was clearly saying "momma." They tried convincing the child to move on and leave this world behind. The team is pretty certain they succeeded with her because she did not return on any audio recordings after that. Another spirit seemed to be very intelligent and responded to the team's questions. He also made it clear he knew he was in a bar when he told the team members to "get him a beer."

If there ever was any doubt about Orton's being haunted, the evidence caught by CSPOT seems to have removed it.

Level Five

Orton's is not the only bar in Wilmington with a few restless souls that may have decided to hang around. In addition to being a nightclub/bar, Level Five is also a theater that provides a wonderful venue for local actors and comedians. It is located at 21 North Front Street and, like the name would suggest, the bar and stage is located on the fifth floor of a five-story building. Oddly enough, the building was initially built as a Masonic temple in 1899. Then, around 1914, the fifth floor was rented out as a theater, which it still one of its primary functions to this day. The first four floors continued to serve the building's original purpose as a Masonic temple until 1981.

Level Five is one of the most popular spots in the Port City. With live entertainment and an open roof bar, it has an atmosphere that other businesses find hard to beat. As is the theme of this book, among the establishment's other extras there are also reports of spectral visitors. Over the years a few customers and performers have found it hard to explain some of their unusual experiences at Level Five.

Damian is a regular at Level Five and is often involved with the theater, causing him to spend time setting up stages and hanging out with friends when there are no crowds of customers. It was on one such evening, while in the theater, that he was setting up the stage without the company of any friends or coworkers. He heard a loud thud come from the auditorium, which was on the other side of the curtain. Curious, he walked to see who was out there and while moving towards the curtain, he heard the distinct sound of feet shuffling only a few feet away. As he opened the curtain Damian was absolutely positive that he was going to see somebody; instead he found no one in or around the stage.

Anthony is another regular at the stage and, like Damian, was on the stage by himself when he found that he actually was not alone in the building. That night he was up on the stage looking out towards the empty seats when he saw a bright flash of light come from nowhere. Then he heard footsteps walking toward him, but shockingly, even as he looked out towards where the sound was coming from, he saw nobody at all.

A short time later, while trying to put what had happened behind him, Anthony heard another phantom sound; it was the unmistakable sound of a little girl talking to someone. Keep in mind that Level Five is a bar, which in general is not a place for children, and add on the late hour. Such a combination of factors makes the presence of any living child very unlikely. Still Anthony searched the premises to see if he could find a stranded child in the theater or bar, but he did not find them and no one he questioned had seen a little girl that evening.

Like so many before, the identity of the little girl's ghost is unknown. There are no reports of any child dying at that location. Still, whoever she is she seems to simply be having fun like everyone else at Level Five.

Fort Fisher

Fort Fisher does not match the image that comes to mind when you hear the word "fort." There are no giant encompassing walls, no cannons; in fact, there is almost nothing. The hastily constructed fort has been completely removed by time and the ever-encroaching Atlantic Ocean, causing it to be little more than an abstract monument to the dead remains of Confederates.

The shoreline of Fort Fisher.

This monument honors the Confederate dead at Fort Fisher.

Only a few feet from the ocean, the Fort Fisher Park is made of sand, green grass, large rock barriers, hills, and a visitor's center. The Confederate Army constructed the fort during the Civil War. It was an earthwork fort made of dirt, rock, and sand. The fort was named after a Confederate officer in the 6th Infantry named Charles F. Fisher, who lost his life in the first Battle of Manasseh on July 21, 1861. At the time, the coastal city of Wilmington was a vital port for the confederacy, second only to Charleston, South Carolina. From its first days in 1861 until its fall to the Union Army in 1865, the fort's main purpose was to protect Wilmington from their enemies, the Union soldiers.

In 1862, a Confederate officer, Colonial Lamb, arrived at Fort Fisher and began to beef up the fort's defense for the Union attack he knew would one day come. By the time he was done, the fort provided a one-mile sea defense and one-third of a mile land defense. As the war became increasingly dismal for the army, troops started being removed from the fort and sent to aid the Confederate Army on different battlefields across the South. The Union army soon began making plans to seize Wilmington after the fall of Mobile, Alabama, in hopes of further crippling the Confederacy by taking this important port city.

By December 1864 the manpower of Fort Fisher had been stripped down and replaced by marginally trained North Carolina locals that were willing to take up arms and defend their homes, but did not have the experience of a veteran army. Military leaders from the Union forces decided that they had finally arrived at the most opportune time to attack the city of Wilmington and its defending fort. Major General Benjamin Butler and Rear Admiral David Dixon Porter, of the Union, attacked the fort for the first time on December 24th; the northern armies were able to land forces, but were routed out by Confederate Major General Robert Hokes. The Union forces withdrew, but not for good. They returned on January 12, 1865, and attacked with fifty-six ships and around 8,000 ground forces. The battle lasted only six hours, resulting with General Whiting surrendering the fort. Wilmington, an important port to the Confederate cause, soon fell along with it, as the fort's guns finally went silent.

Like the blood stained battlefield of Gettysburg, the battlefields around Fort Fisher were a testament to the lost of life on both sides of the war, where men fought and died for their cause. The place, once a proud symbol, had become a cauldron of fear, anger, and death where restless spirits seem to be created.

It was only a few years after the end of the Civil War that visitors to the former Confederate stronghold started to notice peculiar, otherworldly happenings. The earliest reports from the fort occurred less than a decade after the war ended and came from, none other than, Confederate veterans visiting the site. They often reported seeing men in full uniform running around as if they were still in the midst of a battle; like so many other spectral sightings, these men simply vanished in front of them.

The later reports that came around about 1900 were those of a Confederate sentry who seemed to still be standing at his post in a clearing just to the north of the fort. He was always seen standing in his gray Confederate uniform, staring toward the sea. It is likely that many people mistook him for a re-enactor or maybe just someone who could not let the war or the past go. This forgotten solider, by all accounts, seemed completely oblivious to the people who were around, although any attempt to approach him would apparently always cause him to vanish. He has, since his maiden appearance, been seen countless times by tourists, employees, and locals over the decades. I guess no one has told him the Union has come and gone and his duty is done. Although this phantom solider was the first to be widely reported, it was, by no means, the only one that afflicts the fort.

There is a phantom officer at the fort that has been seen numerous times and, unlike the sentry, this ghost seems to be capable and willing to engage in interaction with the living. The officer is most commonly thought to be the ghost of Colonel Lamb, himself; many believe he blamed himself for the fall of the fort, which led to the inevitable fall of the vital port of Wilmington.

He is most often seen walking the beach or the paths near the beach, possibly trying to figure out a different strategy that could have altered the course of the tragic battle that provided another nail in the Confederacy coffin. However, he is not always visually seen making this walk, but his boots are often heard stomping the ground in the same areas whether he is actually seen or not. He has now and then been viewed as he stands by the door at the visitor's center in the park. He looks so much like a living person, with the exception of wearing a Confederate soldier's uniform, which has led people to approach him; assuming he worked at the park and wanting to ask him a question, imagine their shock when he vanishes right before them before they could get the chance!

Now the most interesting story revolving the spectral being that might be Colonel Lamb involves a policeman who was able to get up close and personal with the ghostly man. A member of the Kure beach police department was doing his normal rounds near the fort late at night when he came across a man walking towards Fort Fisher. In and of itself, there is nothing really odd about this in this particular coastal area. People often walk along the beach during the night and some would say it is the best time to do it. So, desiring to be helpful, the officer decided to offer a lift. The man entered his car without saying a single word and only pointed in the direction he wished to go. Judging by the man's Confederate uniform, the cop assumed he was heading towards the fort for some kind of reenactment.

The silent passenger had the officer drive him to directly outside the fort site and then told him to drop him off there. As the man began leaving the car and started to move towards the fort, the officer noticed that this man was slowly fading. Being a little shocked at this, he took off in his car as fast as he could and did not look back. Whichever Confederate ghost the passenger was, he did not seem to mind being given a ride in a piece of modern transportation.

Many visitors often report phantom sounds and smells at the location, most often at night. The most commonly reported sounds are that of battle, gunfire, and artillery being used; some even hear commands being shouted as if in the middle of a battle. This mainly exists along the lines of "open fire" or "hold your ground." There is another phantom sound that does not seem to come from the fort, but actually the Atlantic Ocean and that is the sound of the Union naval bombardment — a few visitors and employees have heard it over the years. Canon fire can be heard off the shore, as well as the sound of exploding shells hitting the ground and the voices of men yelling in agony.

Not all the unnatural noises heard seem to be from an actual battle, but from moments in between. The sound of men marching when there is no one around has been reported near the visitors' center. That may very well be the Confederate troops preparing for battle or possibly the Union after the surrender of the fort. Who is to say? There is a single marcher that can be heard farther from the modern visitor's center and closer to the ageless Atlantic Ocean. He is often thought to be Colonel Lamb and, unlike his full-bodied apparition, this particular manifestation is only detected by a person's ears. The sound of his heavy boots can be heard on the sand and sometimes on the walking path that goes around the site. It is most often thought to be Lamb because much like the one seen walking the beach it would seem whoever was making this march had a lot on his mind.

Jonathan, with his parents and two brothers, was one of the young visitors who attended the site during the summer of 2006. They were standing in front of the visitors' center at the time and had already spent several hours within the park. By this time, it was getting dark outside.

Jonathan's parents were talking to a site employee about the types of events that are often done there.

Jonathan started hearing the sound of men yelling as clear as day and at first assumed it was someone nearby just being obnoxious, but as he looked around he did not see anyone. Still, the yelling got louder and seemed to be coming from all around him. It was soon followed by the sounds of fire and canons going off. He was shocked when he noticed that no one else seemed to hear a thing; his parents and his brothers were all casually talking with the site employee. Soon the noise just stopped around him as creepily as it had started. He did not tell his family until they made it back home, but they did not seem to really believe him and suggested that he had been hearing the ocean. Despite his family's disbelief, Jonathan was sure that what he heard was the Battle of Fort Fisher being spiritually reenacted a century and a half after it had originally taken place.

Like I've previously mentioned, the sounds never have any visual accompaniment, but there have been phantom smells reported that sometimes accompany them. While the sounds of battle are reported and, sometimes a smell of gunpowder floods the air (with or without the sounds), there is a sense that there is a full-scale battle happening all around!

The Visitor's Center, which sits to the side of the fort, is obviously not from around the time of the Civil War, but with the reports of the activity inside and around the building it would seem the ghosts have taken notice of it.

An employee of the center related to me one of the more dramatic events that happened during the summer of 2007 when a member of the staff who no longer works there was locking up the center at the end of the day. He was the last person in the place, which meant that he should have been alone in the building. While checking to make sure all the doors were locked, the most bizarre event began: the brochures began flying off the racks and landed in various places across the lobby! It looked like an invisible angry person was grabbing them and tossing them all around.

This was enough to scare the man beyond words, but the entity (or entities) was not done. It pushed a large donation bin that weighed more than a couple of pounds across the floor with unbelievable force. Quickly, he left the building as it was and had no desire to see what else would happen. The next day the building was in just as much disarray as it had been the night before. What would cause a phantom solider to do this? I am not sure. Maybe he saw something he did not like or possibly he was just trying to get attention or maybe he is just a jerk. Whatever the case may be, the employees who came in the following day and had to clean up the mess were not pleased in the slightest.

A staff member of Fort Fisher gets a shock.

Another friendlier encounter took place during the daytime on another summer day in 2006. A group of tourists who were visiting the site had gone to the Visitor's Center and were in the process of reading bits and pieces of information that were posted on the wall about the battle and the fort. When they got near the glass rear doors, they noticed a Confederate soldier standing on the other side. They assumed it was an employee or maybe a re-enactor, so, without much thought to it, they took their eyes off him for a split second. When they looked back he was gone. Even though his rapid departure was peculiar, the tourists still assumed the more earthbound explanation of who he was until they talked to an employee. Upon asking about him, they were informed that there were no costumed employees on the site at that time. The employee had not seen anyone else walking around in a uniform, and it is kind of hard to miss something like that.

Scott Lambeth and one of his friends were walking along the beach near the fort late one evening when they decided to stop and rest in one of the gazebos that dot the beach. As they sat there talking and admiring the ocean, Scott noticed a woman walking along the shore.

Since it is the beach and it was not uncommon for people to walk along the sand by themselves, even at night, the friends did not think this was an unusual sight. Scott soon realized, however, that this was not a regular person; she was glowing and he could see the ocean behind her as he looked through her. He was in such a daze that he just stared at her as she came closer, not bothering to see if his friend was seeing the strange woman as well.

As she drew to within a few feet of the gazebo she simply vanished. Scott turned around quickly to see if anyone else had witnessed this bizarre event. To his relief, his friend was in just as much astonishment and confusion about what had just happened as he was. Shaken, they decided to head home. As for who this woman was, no one really knows. She may be another causality of the battle or even possibly a spirit of someone who died in that location before or after the tragic event that made the site so famous.

Fort Fisher's primary "haunts" seem to be the residual kind of haunting, which means they are not intelligent beings. They are like a video of a point in time that replays itself over and over and over, with no will, intellect, or conscious thought and no knowledge of anybody outside the scene. These kinds of haunting are generally born out of moments of great emotional stress (which it may surprise you, though it should not, but the Civil War had plenty of) where it is almost as if a person leaves a tiny bit of themselves behind. The phantom marching at Fort Fisher and the sounds of the siege happening again would seem to be the product of a residual haunting.

Still, not all the ghosts are residual; there seem to be a few intelligent hauntings, from those ghosts that take rides from friendly public servants or the ones that decide to trash a Visitor's Center. Now by intelligent, I don't mean they went to the Ivy League schools, but rather they are aware of the living and in some cases try to interact with them.

Fort Fisher is a spot were brave men on both sides of a war gave their lives. It provides a wonderful experience and stands as an important piece of American and North Carolina history. I encourage anyone who finds themselves in the area to make sure to go visit it. Even if you do not encounter the paranormal, being on such an important historical site makes it worth the experience.

Nell Cropsey House

Elizabeth City is a quaint little coastal town, originally founded under the name of Redding in 1793. It was shortly after it was founded that the town was renamed Elizabeth City. It is in this modern era that Elizabeth City is known lovingly as "the harbor of hospitality." This is due to its friendly residents and its complimentary docks open to those who need a place to park their ships for a bit. The city has had a colorful and successful history on the banks of the Pasquotank River, becoming a significant port after the construction of the Dismal Swamp Canal, which made the small town an important center of trade for countless merchants.

It was also the site of a small battle between the Confederate army and the Union on February 10, 1862. Again, it served as the location of another harrowing defeat for the Confederacy, which led Elizabeth City to fall under Union control. This was not before the Confederate Army tried to burn the city to the ground so their enemies could not have it. Only a few blocks were lost before the Union was able to extinguish the flames and save the city.

The city's most famous historic incident involved the murder of a lovely young woman by the name of Ella Maud (Nell) Cropsey. Her father William Cropsey moved from Brooklyn to Elizabeth, along with his family. Their new family home was right on the banks of the Pasquotank. In time, the family found their place fairly easy in the local community.

As for Nell, before long she became involved with a local young man by the name of Jim Wilcox.

Wilcox courted her for nearly three years. It is said that as the years passed Nell became increasingly unhappy with the fact that, after all the time they had been together, Jim had made no marriage proposal; it began to weigh heavily on her. On November 20, 1901, an argument broke out between Nell and Jim; some say it was brought on by Nell's frustration over the lack of a marriage proposal while others say it was Jim's anger over Nell's talking to other men. Regardless of the reasons behind the argument, it is certain that Jim was the last one seen with Nell, as they stepped outside her house to continue their argument in the yard, away from her family.

The Cropsey family soon noticed that Nell had not returned as they were turning in for the evening later that night, yet still did not assume anything was amiss at the time. It was around midnight that Mr. Cropsey and his family was woken by a neighbor screaming that someone was attempting to steal one of the Cropsey's pigs. This, along with a weird thud they had heard earlier, caused the family to inspect what was going on. They did not find anybody outside, but did stumble across Nell's umbrella by the front door as if it had just been placed there.

The family soon realized that even though her umbrella was present Nell was nowhere to be seen. A search of around the house and yard confirmed that she was not there; this led to Nell's family to be consumed by the fear that something untoward had happened to Nell.

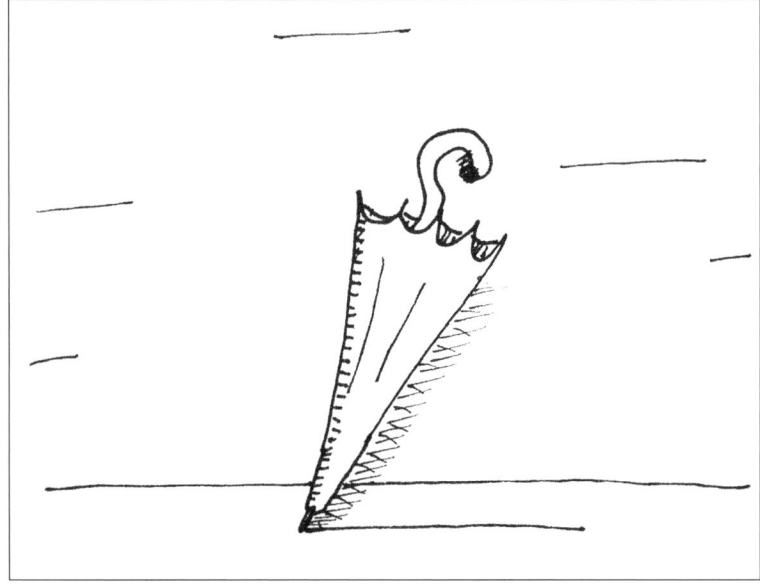

A large search was performed in hopes of finding her, but for thirty-six days it was completely fruitless. On the thirty-seventh day after she had vanished, Nell's lifeless body was found floating in the Pasquotank River with her face down beneath the surface. The coroner determined that the apparent cause of death was blunt trauma to her skull and not been because she had drowned. This made people conclude she had been hit by a large tree branch.

The first and (really) only suspect was Jim Wilcox, the last man to be seen with her. He was quickly arrested and long before the actual trial began, the community had already convicted him. He was put on trial in Pasquotank County; several times during the course of his trial lynch mobs showed up to take justice into their own hands. However, though it was his own daughter who had been killed, Mr. Cropsey refused to take any part in a lynch mob and asked the people to allow justice to be done through the proper channels.

Wilcox was found guilty of first-degree murder in 1902 and sentenced to death, but due to the obvious bias of the town and the trial's constant disruption, he was retried and sentenced to thirty-seven years for second-degree murder.

Jim proclaimed his innocence until his death and swore that when he left Nell that night she was very much alive. There is even some evidence that supports his claim. On Christmas Eve of 1901, Mr. Cropsey received an anonymous letter postmarked from Utica, New York — the letter's author claimed to know what happened to Nell that night. According to the letter, Nell was heading in for the evening after she had finished fighting with Jim. She noticed a man in the process of stealing one of her father's pigs and confronted him, making it clear that she was going to inform her father. In a panic, this would-be pig thief grabbed a nearby tree branch and bashed her in the head. Realizing he had killed her, he took her body, loaded it into a boat, and dumped her body in the lake.

The letter also came with a map that marked where in the lake her body could be found. At the time the letter was dismissed as a cruel joke done in poor taste. People were immovably convinced that Jim Wilcox was guilty. It was barely a week later when Nell's body was found, very close to where it was marked on the map to be. This, along with the later finding that she actually died because of a blunt trauma to the skull, meant that the writer did know a good deal about what had happened that evening.

Even with the information that the letter provided, which only someone who had been present that evening could have known, it was never seriously considered by the authorities and Jim Wilcox was still put on trial twice, and found guilty both times.

The first piece of possibly paranormal events involved with this murder actually happened a few days before Nell's murder even occurred. It involved a premonition by Nell when she had particular vivid dream one evening that, when she awoke, she was convinced meant some kind of misfortune would befall her.

Over the last few years it seems that the spirit of Nell is not at rest, but rather still wanders her family's former home. Folks who visit the historic site sometimes get more than they bargained for: seeing a young woman in white wondering the banks of Pasquotank River right by the home. She, like countless other phantoms, only seems to appear long enough for one good look before vanishing from sight. There is no doubt in many people's minds that this shy specter is Nell, not only because she wears a white dress like the one Nell was found in but because she seems to look out into the river as if it is of great importance to her. Perhaps she is remembering how her earthly remains where disposed of there or maybe she does not believe justice was served and thinks her killer got away. Either way, it is an unsettling thought.

Nell is not the only specter who is reported to still be lurking around; a certain apparition is seen peering from an upstairs window as it looks out toward the lake as well. People quite strongly believe that this ghost is Nell's mother, who in the days after Nell went missing, who was said to spend her time waiting for her daughter to come back to her. It is thought she continues to keep her vigilant watch, even in death, hoping to see Nell one more time. It may be that she left a piece of herself behind once she passed from the world and it is unaware of or refuses to acknowledge her daughter's unfortunate fate.

Chapter Five

The Outerbanks

The Carroll A. Deering

Many people have likely heard of one of history's greatest maritime mysteries: The *Mary Celeste*, a merchant ship that was found still sailing in the Atlantic Ocean at full speed and in perfect condition, but her entire crew mysteriously gone. It was one of those fantastic mysteries I found extremely fascinating in my youth. I never knew that North Carolina had its own equally interesting ship mystery with similar circumstances that occurred forty-nine years after the *Mary Celeste*.

The day February 1, 1921 most likely seemed like any other to the members of the Coast Guard who were stationed at the Outer Banks, near Diamond Shoals. As their day started, it must have been quite a shock to look out into the Atlantic Ocean and see a five-mast schooner crashed into a sand dune not far off shore. The Coast Guard made several attempts to contact anyone on the ship so that they could get permission to board it and provide assistance, but they never received a reply. Increasingly poor weather kept any attempts at rescue at a standstill until February 4th. During that three-day window, they were finally able to find out the ship's name and the place of its launch: it was the *Carroll A. Deering* and it had recently set sail from Norfolk, Virginia, on its way to Rio de Janeiro. Finally, they were also able to receive permission to board the ship from its owners.

As the Coast Guard crew started boarding the ship, they expected to find injured or even dead crewmembers, but instead the deck was empty and seemed to be in perfectly good order, despite the fact it had crashed into the dunes. The rest of the ship was even more of a mystery: like the main deck, the ship was devoid of all crew and seemed free of all signs of foul play, with only one exception — the captain's quarters. It was the only area they had explored on the vessel that appeared to have been rummaged through. All the other rooms on the ship were in no obvious disarray and in the mess hall, there was still uneaten food sitting on the table.

Then they found that most all of the documents had been removed from the ship as well as the navigation equipment. They also found that the steering mechanism had been smashed to shards, as if to prevent anyone from controlling the ship. The lifeboats were also nowhere on the ship, instigating speculation that the vessel had been abandoned for some unknown reason, but this did not explain the destruction of essential equipment onboard the ship.

As an investigation ensued so did conspiracy theories about what had happened to the crew. Some believed that some kind of disease overtook them and they were forced to flee the ship before they succumbed to it. This theory is flawed because, if it had been a disease of some kind, some already infected crewmembers would have been left behind. Still, there were others that believed pirates had taken the crew for some nefarious reason while others posed the theory that a mutiny had taken place on the vessel. Most people consider the mutiny theory to explain the likeliest scenario of what happened on the ship, especially as witnesses and facts came forward in the days and weeks after it was found.

The *Deering* set off from Bath, Maine, destined for Rio de Janeiro with a shipment of coal. She was originally captained by William H. Merritt, but after only short time into their voyage he became seriously ill. Forced to disembark in Lewis, Delaware, Captain Merritt was replaced as soon as possible. His replacement was an experienced captain, W. B. Wormell, who was sixty-six years old at the time; the fact that he was of advanced age made the crew uneasy.

After the ship reached Rio, the crew was given leave and Wormell took the time to catch up with Captain Goodwin, a friend who happened to be in the same port. It was while drinking with him that Wormell foolishly made the statement that he mistrusted the *Deering's* crew. Later on, Wormell's first mate spoke with a Captain Norton and voiced his misgivings about Wormell, claiming he was too controlling on the ship and his eyesight was so poor that he was useless when it came to navigation. Later on Norton, along with others, overheard Mclellan declare, "I'll get that captain before we get to Norfolk, I will!"

As the *Deering* made its way back toward Norfolk, the crew was making very good time...at least until January 23rd. From the 23rd to the 29th, the *Deering* only traveled eighty miles, from Cape Fear to Cape Lookout.

The citizens of Bridgetown, which was located on the Outer Banks, came forward with an unusual claim. Some citizens swore, as the ship passed their town on the 23rd, that they heard the sound of a loud ruckus on the deck. It culminated in someone screaming, "Get the old man." Many think this "old man" label was probably referring to Captain Wormell, who may have been in trouble with his crew at the time.

A few days later a lightship, which works as a makeshift lighthouse, was moored off Cape Lookout. Its captain, who went by the name Jacobson, found something odd about the ship and her crew as they sailed by him. As he looked at the deck, he noticed that some of the *Deering's* crew seemed to be aimlessly shuffling around; one man with a bull horn called over to the light ship and claimed that the *Deering* had lost its anchor in a recent storm and wanted all ships to be warned and give it a wide berth so there would be no collisions.

The crew of the lightship made two observations about what they saw on this curious encounter. One was the man with the bull horn did not look like an officer in any way, shape, or form; in fact no one they saw looked like an officer. The other thing that struck them as curious was the claim of losing an anchor in a storm because no powerful storms had been the area for a good amount of time.

The last thing to surface that seemed to indicate an unsavory end to the captain's career, in particular, was the only log found still onboard. Wormell had signed all entries since the day he came aboard, yet on the 23rd and the days after, the signatures were noticeably different. Even Wormell's daughter, after she examined it, declared, "That is not my father's signature!"

The story in itself is a fascinating piece of North Carolina history with a mystery that will probably never been given a definitive answer. The crew was never heard of again, save for a message stuffed into a bottle that allegedly washed up on shore April 1, 1921. A man by the name of Christopher Columbus Gray supposedly found it on the beach as he was strolling along it and immediately handed it over to the proper authorities. The note's handwriting was viewed by Captain Wormell's daughter, who said it was the handwriting of an engineer on-board named Bates.

The note, which pointed to piracy as the fate of the *Deering*, said this:

> *Deering* captured by oil burning boat something like chaser taking off everything handcuffing crew, crew hiding all over ship, no chance to make escape, finder please notify headquarters *Deering*.

That note should have put an official explanation to the disappearance of the crew, but many were not convinced in its sincerity and eventually, after some pressure Mr. Gray admitted the note was a fake of his own making. He had planned to take advantage of the crew's disappearance to perpetuate his own designs.

The active investigation ended about a year after the ship was found crashed into the Diamond Shoals with no certain answer to what had happened; it would seem the crew's fate would be lost with the ages.

The fact that the crew of the *Deering* was never heard from again is not the only reason most people believe that all or most of them perished. At night, off the Diamond Shoals, phantom screams can be heard coming from the direction of the ocean. Many believe that, possibly crashing on Diamond Shoals, the crew evacuated the ship only to be capsized by the unfriendly weather at the time.

While walking the shoreline in a casual laid back mood, breathing in the wonderful sea air, people have heard the very loud and real screams of help from men in the sea! The natural reaction is to locate the source of the pleas, yet none can ever be found. With the exception of the blue waves crashing on the shore, the ocean is as calm as can be. There are no men splashing in great distress, no bodies and no signs of harrowed ship.

It is possible that if they did, in fact, abandon the ship to cover up for the mutiny the poor weather could have caused their lifeboat to be taken by the ocean. Now they still haunt those waters, screaming for a rescue that will never come.

Blackbeard

Edward Teach or, as he is better known, Blackbeard, is the infamous pirate whose tale is woven into the history of the Carolinas. He is one of maritime history's most fearsome high seas bandit and he is strongly connected with North Carolina because he used, what was at the time, the British colony of North Carolina, specifically Ocracoke Island, as his base of operations for much of his pirating career.

Blackbeard.

What made Blackbeard stand out from the rest of his ilk? Why is he remembered so well while others are lost to pages of history? Well, some of the reasons are attributed to his well-known but terrifying appearance and his seemingly unending streaks of successful attacks. Another reason may be his somewhat contradictory gentleman-like ways. Blackbeard was not afraid to take a life, not even for a second, yet he was known to display, what at the time could best be called, mercy to his captives and even his crew. If people were willing to surrender their valuables without a fight, he would usually let them go unharmed.

This is not saying he should apply for sainthood, but those who dedicate their lives to robbing and killing are very seldom known to display any compassion towards their enemies. It was his ability to do this that led to the belief that, before his pirating days, Edward Teach was an English gentleman. If so, for some reason he seemed to have gotten bored with class and wealth and turned to an illustrious life of pillaging and plundering, though there is little proof of this and it's really just speculation.

It is hard to believe that his iconic stranglehold of terror on the east coast merely lasted two years, beginning in 1716. He made his home in the Outerbanks where he was blessed with the perfect location to attack and rob merchant vessels that were heading to the colonies. In 1717, he even captured a 26-gun British ship called the *Concorde* (a slave ship), but he was not happy with two things about the ship: the name and the meager twenty-six cannons it was equipped with. He renamed her *Queen Anne's Revenge* and added fourteen more guns, which brought the cannons to a respectable count of forty.

When it came to pirating, Blackbeard was a pro; it can safely be said that if he set his eye on a "prize" he would have it before he could blink. He put large amounts of work into keeping his crew ready for battle and stayed one step ahead of British naval forces on the Carolina coast that wanted to put an end to him.

Blackbeard had the art of looking scary down; this hopefully will not come as a shock to anyone, but he did have a very long black beard. What some may not know is, during battles he would often put fuses in his beard and light them; the smoke flowing from his beard would fill his enemies with fear and make him seem supernatural. This tactic contributed to them usually losing their nerve to fight him. I, of course, would make some comment about how burning hair smelt but it was the early 1700s so everything smelled horribly already.

Blackbeard got away with pillaging and many other nefarious deeds, which included kidnapping (once even taking a councilman and his son hostage in exchange for medical supplies), murder, and the overall disturbance of the peace. Oddly enough, the residents of North Carolina benefited from his robbing; the items stolen from merchants where often sold for a whole lot less than the merchant had been selling, almost like the discount stores of our day, albeit a little scarier.

It was not until the year 1718 that he finally met his fate, and in a way it's extremely funny. It was not the raping and pillaging, murders or kidnapping that would cause the hammer to come down on him. Instead it was a noise complaint by his neighbors that would be his undoing.

It was shortly after marrying his newest wife (he has been reported as having as many as twelve) and being semi-retired from his pirating life that Blackbeard threw a massive party; bonfires, drinking and no shortage of some disreputable individuals were in attendance. This equivalent of a pirate kegger went on for several days and the noise was so bad that a handful of nearby Virginia residents decided that enough was enough. So they went to inform the governor of Virginia, Alexander Spotswood, of the problem. Realizing the benefits and glory of removing Blackbeard from the seven seas, he was quick to act.

He hired a British officer named Robert Maynard, who was given command of the naval vessel *Jane,* which was a small sloop. A Mr. Hyde commanded the sloop Ranger. Maynard's orders were to simply capture Blackbeard so he could be but on trial, but things would not work out as originally planned.

Maynard and his ships had no trouble locating the infamous pirate near his camp at Ocracoke; they arrived later in the day on November 21 and decided to wait for morning when the tide would come in before making any kind of move to capture the infamous pirate. The *Jane* and *Ranger* were at a distinct disadvantage to *The Adventure*; they had no heavy guns aboard, only the small arms that the crew carried, while *The Adventure* was heavily armed. On the reverse side, *The Adventure* had only nineteen pirates onboard and Blackbeard, along with the majority of his crew, had spent the previous evening drinking heavily.

As soon as the pirates were aware of the approaching ships, they set sail and prepared to engage their enemies, much like they had done many times before. The ship used some fast maneuvering (fast maneuvering by those days standards) and was able to cause the sloops to run aground in shallow waters, but both the *Jane* and *Ranger* were able to break free with the help of the rising tide and the work of their tireless crew.

Blackbeard ordered a volley of canon fire launched at the sloops; this attack resulted in the death of crewmembers on both ships along with the commander of the *Ranger*, Mr. Hyde. This put the *Ranger* out of the pursuit, but Maynard decided to try to outsmart the cunning pirate as opposed to out-passing him, using the damage and smoke to put up a ruse and take advantage of the infamous pirate's brashness.

Knowing the pirate could not resist boarding the ship to finish off his pursuers if he thought their numbers had been decimated by the canon fire, Maynard ordered all but two of his men to hide below deck. The ship looked as if the crew had been almost entirely killed or at least put out of commission when Blackbeard fell for the bait. Along with ten of his men, the pirate boarded the ship with plans of dispatching the remaining members of the crew, but unfortunately discovered that they were at an insurmountable disadvantage when Maynard and his crew swarmed the deck. In a scene fit for Hollywood, Blackbeard and Maynard met face-to-face in battle while their crews fought all around them.

It was no surprise that Maynard was unable to best Blackbeard in a sword fight; he even suffered a deep wound to his hands in his attempt to fight, but unwilling to be defeated, Maynard did the only thing he could do to save his life — he pulled out his pistol and shot Blackbeard just as Blackbeard prepared to finish him off. This did not stop the terror off the Carolina coast and, if not for the fact that a member of the *Jane's* crew soon joined in on attacking Blackbeard, Maynard would have died at the wounded pirate's deadly hands.

It would take a grand total of five shots and twenty stab wounds to finally cause Blackbeard to fall to the deck in a puddle of his own blood. The reasons for what happened next is debatable, but Maynard had Blackbeard's head cut off and placed on the *Jane's* bowsprit and then ordered that the pirate's body be tossed overboard. Most reports say that he had his head cut off to make sure he was actually deceased; others say it was to give him a trophy when he went triumphantly back to Virginia.

It was the removal of his head that is the focal point of almost all the ghost stories revolving around Blackbeard's earthbound spirit. After all a guy like that wouldn't let a little thing like being decapitated slow him down, right?

The first of many claims of the paranormal involving the ghost of Blackbeard came only a matter of minutes after his death at the hands of the *Jane's* crew, which claimed that after his headless body was tossed into the Atlantic it began to swim around the ship multiple times. Some even said his severed head let out an unearthly shriek on the deck, probably to mock Maynard's belief that he had won and fill the enemy crew with one last swelling of fear. It would seem that death has not stopped his legend or his restless spirit; since the time of his demise people have reported encounters with this headless ghost.

Ocracoke Island, near where the battle took place, is now known as Teach's Hole in honor of Edward Teach and has several ghostly apparitions, all of which are believed to be the work of Blackbeard's angry spirit. Much like his physical body was rumored to have done after it was tossed overboard the *Jane* all those years ago, a lot of folks now claim to see his headless body just offshore, swimming in fast paced laps as it gives off an unearthly glow. His headless ghost has even been reported to leave the water carrying a lantern and walk the beaches, either looking for his head or revenge on those who took it from him. It is said that even on the most hot summer evening the temperature will drop to a frigid point whenever he manifests near the beach.

Blackbeard's final fight.

Sometimes the strange happenings are not that of a physical being, but of sounds and eerie unexplained lights. People often see what they describe as an unearthly light glowing just under the surface of the waves, or, at others times, right above it. It is most often seen as almost like light emitting spheres that seem to be vibrating. Others have described seeing a luminescent mist coming from the ocean that reaches toward the shore like a tentacle from the depths. This is sometimes accompanied by terrifying laughter; all who hear it are convinced that it is that of North Carolina's most infamous pirate, Edward Teach, mocking their fear and possibly even death itself.

Blackbeard's ghost is not as common as he once was; it is a rarity these days for people to report any kind of encounter with him. Still he is permanently intertwined within the history and lore of the Tar Heel State, so the stories of his pirating escapades and his haunting will be around forever, even if his soul is finally at rest.

Cape Hatteras

One of the things that North Carolina is best known for is the Cape Hatteras Lighthouse. Known for being one of the first lighthouses in the United States, it now stands at 203 feet, making it the tallest one in the country. It can be seen sporting a black and white spiral strip that has been lovingly dubbed the "big barber poll."

The original lighthouse was constructed in 1803 because of the severe danger of the waters near Hatteras beach, which are known as the Diamond Shoals. Due to the cold Labrador stream from the north and the warm gulf steam, it watches over some extremely dangerous water currents that, combined with the sandbars, have helped the graveyard of the Atlantic claim over 2,000 ships and send crews and passengers to their watery graves.

By the start of the Civil War, the original lighthouse had become known for being very ineffective at saving ships. Its short height and poor light quality made it almost completely useless, so in 1873 a new one was built; it is the one that still stands today and is a much taller structure that projects quite a bit better lighting. The new improvements did not stop ships from falling victim to the waters altogether, but it cut the numbers down.

Today Hatteras Lighthouse does not actually stand where it was constructed; it was moved in 1999 to save it from the fast encroaching Atlantic Ocean. She is open to the public almost every day of the year and runs an informative visitor center. Many folks come to the site to look upon the impressive structure and learn a little history at the same time.

Many a person who visits the lighthouse has claimed to hear doomed souls screaming for help or struggling in the nearby water only to stop without explanation within moments. People on the beach at night will do more then hear these lost souls at times, odd luminescent mist are seen around the shore, sometimes looking like a glowing fog, but at others taking on the shape of a featureless human being walking towards the shore.

One of the area's most famous ghosts walks the beach by the lighthouse during the late nocturnal hours. She has been seen numerous times for well over a hundred years; a highly elegant looking young woman, with her hair twisted in a bun, and clothed in a white dress, she is normally seen walking the Hatteras beach with a genuinely mournful look on her face. She will vanish when anyone tries to draw near her. She is said to give off an unearthly glow just like the areas other haunts, leaving no mark on the beach's sand or making any noise as she walks down her path.

This ghost is not only a well known spook but it is widely believed to be the daughter of one of America's most infamous and earliest political figures, Aaron Burr, who was the third vice president of the United States. He killed John Hamilton in a duel and plotted building his own empire in what was a then Spanish controlled land. His daughter was a beautiful young woman by the name of Theodosia Burr Alston.

Theodosia had a very different childhood than most girls of her time. Her father had stressed education and took a strong interest in making sure she was learning everything she could to be self-reliant. It should be no surprise that many families of the time thought a girl's education should not extend beyond cooking, cleaning, and being a hostess, but Aaron Burr made sure she learned proper writing style and mathematics. In exchange for his desire to give her a proper mind, she was a fiercely loyal daughter, staying by his side in his most troubling spots, which included Burr being put on trial in 1807 for treason.

On February 2, 1801 she married the governor Joseph Alston of South Carolina and would set the precedent for countless newlyweds after them by honeymooning at Niagara Falls. She would begin her own family with Joseph, but always remand loyal to her father even after he departed to Europe when he was found innocent of his treason charges.

Her father would not come back until July 1812 and sent word to his daughter in South Carolina that he wished to see her. She could not come right away; her son died only a month shy of her father's return and she was still gripped with depression. She waited until the end of December to try and see him. She left Georgetown, South Carolina, on December 31st by method of a schooner known as the *Patriot*; the day the ship sailed out of that port would be the last that anyone would see it or anyone who had ridden upon it. Sadly, Theodosia was never reunited with her father.

The theories of the ship's fate have been emerging since the very first days that followed its disappearance, but there are two that hold the strongest possibility of being the correct one. The *Patriot* could have fallen to the very real and dangerous threat of group of despicable scavengers known as the "wreckers," a group of men that were based near Nags Head beach. These men took advantage of the dangers of the waters that claimed so many ships; they waited for a vessel to suffer an ill-fate and, as the debris washed ashore, they would pick it clean and profit off the death.

Yet sometimes, despite the dangers of the nearby waters, they would find themselves with no wrecked ships to pillage, so they simply arranged for some. They tied a lantern to a mule's neck and, deviously, they would walk the animal back and forth along the shoreline. In the dark night, as ships sail the ocean, a lantern on shore moving back and forth would very strongly resemble a lantern on a ship that was being tossed about by the rough waves. Ships passing by would often fall for this horribly, ruthless trick, they would attempt to lend assistance not knowing that they were sailing right into the graveyard of the Atlantic right into a trap.

The ship would wreck and the parasites swarmed to the vessel in rowboats; they would show no mercy to the surviving crew and passengers, killing all those they came across. It was a terrible fate, but not that uncommon in those days for a ship to meet such a horrific end and the *Patriot* happened to be in the vicinity of where the Wreckers operated.

Another even more common fate that befell ships was to be done in by the unfeeling, and unmerciful elements. Some records seem to point to that being a possible finale for the unfortunate ship.

During the period the *Patriot* vanished, a war was going on between America and England: the War of 1812. Not too far from the Outer Banks, a British blockade fleet was located near the coast of North Carolina. Records that have been found from that fleet mention a particularly terrible storm that began on January 2nd and lasted until the 3rd. The *Patriot*, had she been going at her normal pace, would have almost definitely run into this storm and because it was a smaller ship, it could have been destroyed. Some even say that Theodosia's body was found washed up on shore in Norfolk, Virginia, in early 1813. A man named J. A. Elliott told the tale near the end of his life in 1910, saying the body of a young and obviously well-to-do girl did wash up on shore shortly after the ship's disappearance and was eventually buried in a small grave on his farm.

No matter the fate of the *Patriot* or of Theodosia's mortal remains, it would seem her spirit (or one that resembles her) continues to this day to walk the shorelines of Cape Hatteras, possibly in a daze about her death or maybe still trying to make her way to her father whom she never arrived to see.